FOXES, [illegible]

When the Burkett fami[illegible] their small home to all [illegible] [th]ey little dreamed that *they* [illegible] move out!

Here is the author's own lively account of a few of the most memorable – and amusing – visitors to the Burkett household. The problems of feeding a kingfisher who will eat only *live* fish, the hazards of sharing your bath with a thrush and your bed with a rabbit – these are just some of the incidents in a book about running a home for animals – without them running you!

Also available in the Target series:

THAT MAD, BAD BADGER Molly Burkett
ABANDONED! G. D. Griffiths
A SKUNK IN THE FAMILY Constance Taber Colby
TEMBA DAWN, MY CALF Alec Lea
BENJI Alison Thomas

FOXES, OWLS AND ALL

Lively, humorous tales of an animal-crazy household

Molly Burkett

A TARGET BOOK
published by
the Paperback Division of
W. H. ALLEN & Co. Ltd.

A Target Book
Published in 1977
by the Paperback Division of W. H. Allen & Co. Ltd
A Howard & Wyndham Company
123 King Street, London W6 9JG

Published simultaneously in Great Britain by
Allan Wingate (Publishers) Ltd, 1977

Printed in Great Britain by
Richard Clay (The Chaucer Press) Ltd, Bungay, Suffolk

ISBN 0 426 11770 0

Contents

Foreword

By Andrew Greenwood, M.A.vet., M.B., M.R.C.V.S.

Whether it be as a result of increasing public interest in wildlife, or of greater pressures on animals and their environment, there is now an urgent demand for active conservation in Britain. For many people conservation means subscribing to some organisation which seeks to preserve wildlife habitat away from human interference. For too many others it means dealing with the results of that interference – the harsh reality of an oiled puffin struggling on the beach or an injured badger dying in a roadside ditch, which induces a desperate feeling of helplessness and guilt.

Molly Burkett and her family spend their time and energy coping with just this problem. On behalf of the rest of us they apply their skill and patience to help individual bird or animal casualties, nursing them back to health and freedom, and provide a secure and comfortable home for those which can never return to the wild. *Foxes, Owls and All* covers every aspect of animal care – not just the medical and behavioural difficulties, but the disruptions of normal life, late hours and constant inconvenience which prevent most people from undertaking such responsibilities. It is their ready acceptance of this way of life, as well as their knowledge and compassion, which makes the Burketts such a positive force for conservation.

CHAPTER ONE: The Beginning

The middle-aged lady came panting into the room and handed John a shoe box which had been carefully tied with pink ribbon. We were in the middle of dinner and stopped to stare at her, our forks poised in front of our mouths. We had not heard her come in; the bell had not rung; no one had rattled the door knocker. She had simply appeared in the middle of our dining room. John untied the ribbon and carefully removed the box lid. We all peered inquisitively inside, a dead bat lay on a piece of tissue paper.

We often saw Miss Buller after that. She seemed to develop the habit of appearing at the most unexpected time with pathetic victims of road accidents. If the injured animal was not already dead, it was usually breathing its last. The difficulty was that when John explained that there was little chance of the creature recovering, she would start to cry and it was generally a long time before she felt well enough for us to take her home. This went on for the entire summer – until she changed her interest to second-hand cars. The last time we saw her, she had five of them jammed into her front garden, none of which would go.

The thing was that Miss Buller cared. She hated seeing small birds and animals suffer, and she wanted to do something about it. Her feelings were not very different from our own when we started taking in wild animals which were in need of care. We never planned to become so involved with wildlife: it just seemed to happen. When we married in 1954, myxomatosis was at its height. As we walked through the countryside that summer we saw rabbits suffering and dying in their thousands. Until that time rabbits had been as much a part of the English countryside as oak trees and wood pigeons. It was difficult to pass a field without seeing rabbits in those days, giving their positions away with a white flash from the underneaths of their fluffy round tails as they lolloped towards the hedgerows. Rabbits were an essential part of country life. Countrymen shot and trapped them, ate the meat and sold the skins. Predators – foxes, badgers and buzzards – hunted the rabbit: they were part of the food chain.

The rabbit's only fault was that there were too many of them and that consequently they ate too much. They were eating away the farmer's profits. In order to cut the problem down to size, myxomatosis was introduced: the happy, gambolling animals which once dotted the countryside were reduced to crawling, blinded objects, their heads covered with suppurating sores, their eyes caked and weeping. As the disease penetrated their brains, they would turn round and round, circling aimlessly.

For me, myxomatosis has been the greatest misuse of knowledge and science in this century. To see those rabbits as we saw them was the most horrifying and ugly sight. It was equally tragic that there was no way of helping them: only death could do that.

John and I wanted to help. It worried us that animals could suffer as the rabbits were suffering in 1954 and we wanted to do something about it. A rabbit was one of the first animals we received. A few months later we were asked to take a kestrel: Cully was our first bird.

That first year we had seven patients; the next year we received seventy-seven, and from then on we lost count. Our animal centre became like Topsy: it 'just growed'. Now, at any one time, we expect to have between two and three hundred birds and animals on the premises, although we do receive far more birds, presumably because there are more of them to be injured in the first place.

From the beginning our aim has been not only to care for the animal but to get it fit enough to return to the wild. There have been two different branches of animal husbandry which we have studied: animal care and animal rehabilitation. There is so much more involved than getting an animal fit, taking it out into the countryside and letting it go. An animal which has become used to shelter and food at regular times is not going to become a wild creature as soon as it sees green fields and trees. It has to adapt to these things, and adaptation can take a long time – it can sometimes be as long as two years before an animal becomes self-reliant. Often it has to be taught to recognize food: a finch, for example, which has found its food in a bowl will not immediately recognize seed which grows on a stalk; owls which have been fed on butcher's meat are not going to recognize their meal when it is wrapped up in fur and scurries through the undergrowth in the form of a mouse! Sometimes animals become so used to human beings and unnatural surroundings that they are able neither to recognize their own kind nor to settle down in their natural environment. Sometimes they just do not want to go back to the wild; often they become too tame. You can make a wild bird tame but you can *never* make a truly tame one wild.

We will accept any wild bird or animal on condition that it is released to the wild when and if we think it is fit. We have had a certain amount of success in the last twenty-four years, and we have learned a good deal. All we try to do is give the creatures that come to us another chance, a chance of life and, in some cases, a chance of freedom. We like to stop sometimes and think that we have given that chance to well over two thousand creatures. We know that our two children, St John and Sophie, have become just as interested and involved in the work as we have ourselves.

CHAPTER TWO: The Kingfisher

Sometimes one sees a miracle. The kestrel which had been sent up from Cornwall lay in its box as though dead. It might well have been. It had lost all power of movement except for the ability to move its head from side to side. We wondered if it was fair to keep it alive: it did not seem to have much of an existence lying there like that. But even while we were standing there, looking at it, making up our minds, that bird struggled and tried to move. So we gave it a chance. It was a long, slow job but gradually it improved and was coaxed into flight again.

Two years to the day after we had received that kestrel, it spread its wings and circled higher into the sky. It allowed the breeze to carry it across to a field which had been harvested and where the stubble stood like a brittle carpet. There it hovered and, as we watched, it folded its wings into its body and dived down towards the ground, at something his sharp eyes had seen. Then it lifted into the air again and hovered once more further down the valley. It was a wild bird again. Remembering the pathetic state that bird had been in when it had arrived all that time ago, how can one doubt that miracles do happen?

The story of the old badger is similar. He had been run over by a lorry in Derbyshire. It was only by chance that a family stopped to look at him and realized that he was still alive. The lorry had gone right over his back and gouged out a piece of flesh the length of his spine. He was in a dreadful mess. Because the wound was on his spine, his whole nervous system was affected, his hindquarters were completely paralysed, and he only had limited movement in his front legs. The family which had found him would have liked to look after the animal themselves and had kept him for a few days before they brought him to us. They told us honestly that they could not afford the vet's bills and they knew the badger needed proper treatment.

How I wish other people were as honest. People often keep birds or animals two or three weeks before they bring them to us, and they hardly ever think of taking them to the vet. By then it is often too late. Once the creature has been cut, infection has had a chance to get in; if it has broken a limb, the ends of the bones will have begun to die. People who break a leg do not sit with it like that for a couple of weeks before they decide to do something about it. Animal bones are made of the same stuff, and need the same priorities. We can often save the animal: sometimes the vet will pin the bone, putting a piece of metal between the two bone ends and holding it in that way; but the longer it is left the more remote are the chances of getting it fit enough to return to its own environment and its own natural life.

We thought that even the few days these people had kept the badger had been too long. The flesh near the wound was discoloured and it smelt. We thought that where the flesh had begun to rot and die gangrene had set in. We took it straight to the vet fully expecting him to tell us that it was not fair to keep the animal alive.

It was a long time before he could give us any

decision at all. Although that badger's body was pretty useless, its head certainly was not. He growled with a menace that sent shivers down my back when we put him on the table. He meant it too because when Colin, the vet, touched him, he whipped his head round and snapped, catching hold of his arm. He shook his head and ripped the sleeve of Colin's jacket. Colin jumped back and studied that badger warily. Then he said, 'You keep him still and I'll look at him.'

Easier said than done! As soon as we approached, the animal snapped out and, although he lay there still and sick, he had the ability to move his head with amazing speed and accuracy. Badgers are formidable animals at the best of times, but if you try and put one of them on an operating table for an examination, it can become fearfully aggressive! (A lesson which we learnt that day.) In the end we had to check the badger a bit at a time.

Colin's operating table had a handle which enabled him to adjust the top to a convenient height. This time he wanted it as high as it would go. John and St John between them held the badger still, putting a blanket over him and holding him down firmly. Colin and I sat on the floor under the black operating table and looked at the badger a piece at a time as the others eased first one leg and then the other over the edge of the table top. We ran into difficulties when we had to examine the cut on the top of his head – but we managed. That animal had taken a terrific knock; in fact, it seemed a wonder that he had survived at all. Where he had not been actually cut by the lorry, he had had the gravel from the road ground into his body.

Nine months to the day that we received that badger, he trotted off through the woods without a backward glance. He still dragged one of his back legs a little but that was the only sign of his accident. He went through that wood, only pausing to give himself a shake and a scratch behind his ear as if to say, 'Right, that's got that lot out of my hair,' before he trotted on. When we thought of the dreadful state he had been in when he came into the centre, and compared it with this animal going back to his own world without a care, can there be any doubt that miracles do happen?

Our first kingfisher gave us a similar sense of wonder. It was not that it made a miraculous recovery; it was the sheer beauty of the bird that took our breath away. I had expected a brightly coloured bird when I took it from the box, but I was not prepared for the sheer iridescent qualities of those colours.

Kingfishers have fascinated me since I was a small child. I have wasted hours watching them swooping from one vantage point to another, the bright flashes of colour giving their position away. I like to see the cheeky way they bob, turning their heads first to one side, and then the other to catch the movement of the fish in the water below. Without doubt it is their colour which makes them so attractive.

This bird in my hand seemed much brighter than the one which I had observed in the wild. It was really gay with its deep red breast and turquoise head and wings. The white patches on its neck seemed to accentuate the gaiety of its colours. Its feathers had a translucent quality that seemed to reflect different colours and different shades. When it stretched its wings, the blue on its back shimmered with the light, making the rest of it seem dull by comparison.

It was smaller than I had expected it to be but then birds look smaller when they are sitting still than they do when in flight. It was about six inches in length, although its sharp, dagger-like beak made it appear longer still.

We had collected the kingfisher from the Wingates, who ran the pet shop in Winchester. A lady had gone into the shop and, rather than take a bird out of the door, she had brought one in; the kingfisher lay in a sorry huddle at the bottom of her basket. It seemed very shocked and made no attempt to move. The lady told us that, while walking round the shopping arcade, she had seen a group of women looking at something on the ground. It was the kingfisher. The bird was trying helplessly to spread its wings, but every time it struggled to fly, a twisted left wing caused it to fall to the ground again. It repeated this exercise half a dozen time before the lady bent down, picked it up and took it into the pet shop.

'I do hope you can come soon,' Mrs Wingate said to me anxiously over the phone. 'It'll only eat live food, you know. We are trying to establish a fish farm and this bird's eating all our profits.'

We examined the bird carefully when we collected it. Its wing was indeed badly swollen and discoloured – but we did not think it was broken.

'It's just a bad sprain,' John said. 'It will be flying by the end of the week. It only needs a day or two's rest.'

These were the most optimistic words he ever uttered. Three weeks later that bird was still with us, still not using its wing properly and still having us running round in circles all day trying to satisfy its appetite.

We learned a lot about kingfishers in those three weeks. The first and most important discovery was that Mrs Wingate was right. Kingfishers will only eat live food. However tempting we made its meal, that bird would not touch it unless it was swimming gaily round a bowl of water.

We tried all kinds of tricks but the bird did not fall for any of them. We cut slivers of meat and fish that we thought looked like the real thing: the kingfisher thought otherwise. St John fixed up a contraption with a dish of water, pulleys and bits of string. The idea was that when he pulled the string, the dish moved up and down, and this in turn made the water stir, with the result that the pieces of meat inside it moved and, in doing so, looked like fish swimming round. At least, that was the idea. It was not a success. Part of the trouble was that St John had arranged the string so that he could sit in the armchair, watch television *and* rock the dish at the same time. This meant that the string stretched across the doorway with the result that the dinner twice finished up in a heap on the hearth rug when I happened to trip head first over his invention.

The other drawback was that the kingfisher did not enter into the spirit of the thing. It loved to watch the pieces of moving string, and would study them with great interest, bobbing its head up and down and turning full on one side to get a better look. Unfortunately, it didn't show the slightest interest in the food which was swilling about in its cage. And that was another problem: it was difficult to keep the thing just rocking. The movement tended to get more and more violent until everyone and everything within reach had been sprayed with the fishy-smelling water – and sometimes a few pieces of raw fish and meat into the bargain! St John had a brainwave: it would be more successful if he worked the whole thing by electricity. After he had fused all the lights, we gave up and resorted to force-feeding...

In general, we are always reluctant to force-feed an animal. We think it can break down the trust between animals and human beings. In the case of that kingfisher, however, we had no choice.

Birds have unusual tongues. At the back they have a backward-facing two-pronged fork. When you put the food into the bird's beak, you must be sure to get it behind this fork. When the bird closes its beak, that fork automatically goes to the back of the mouth and pushes the food down into the crop. If the food is liquid, you have to be doubly careful: there is also a hole at the top of the throat, and this is its airhole. If you do not get the food far enough back, you can block this hole and suffocate the bird; alternatively, if the food is liquid, it can disappear down the hole and collect in the bird's lungs and drown it.

Fortunately, feeding that kingfisher was a relatively easy job. It had an enormous gape for a bird of its size. When it opened its beak, the aperture was so big that I could put my finger down its throat with ease. All I had to do was put the food in the bird's beak. One quick swallow and he would be ready for more. Nor did he seem to object to being handled – in fact, from the way in which he would take time off to have a good look round him before he swallowed another mouthful, you would think that he was having the time of his life!

Live food was a necessity. Force-feeding is all very well, but it can only be a temporary measure. You must not let a bird become so accustomed to being fed that he takes it for granted. If that happens, it will be very difficult to get him to resume the feeding habits that are going to be necessary if he is to survive in the wild. Goldfish at fifteen pence each were out – far too expensive! We did treat him to a couple but they disappeared in the blink of an eye!

I decided that there was nothing else for it: I would have to return to the days I thought I had left behind years ago, and start fishing for tiddlers ...

That was easier said than done. We still lived in Hampshire then, and river banks there are guarded jealously. Fishing rights in that area are some of the most expensive in the world. I guessed the water bailiff would probably turn a blind eye to a small boy with his fishing net, but I had no doubt at all what his reactions would be to a well-built woman following the same activity.

The first river bailiff I spoke to was very helpful. He promised to ask a couple of boys from the village to fish me out a few. If I would like to call round that evening he would have them ready. That suited us fine. It just happened that we had to pass his door on our way to a friend's silver wedding party. We promised to collect them on the way. I was delighted when I saw the bucketful of river life those two boys had found for us. There were at least a hundred minnows swimming round as well as – er – a number of other things ... We paid our fifty pence willingly and marched triumphantly back to the car with the slopping bucket.

We both thought of the snag at the same time. How do you carry a bucketful of assorted river life in a car – and particularly when you are wearing evening dress? We never did find out. I doubt if we travelled more than five miles an hour (much to the annoyance of the queue of cars behind us). Every time we went round a corner or hit a bump in the road, I collected another lapful of assorted river life. I kept my fingers crossed all evening that the other guests would put the peculiar smell down to some new kind of perfume.

If I had second thoughts about those fish, the kingfisher certainly did not. He went into action straight away – just like a clockwork toy. Up, down, up, down, up, down, he bobbed his head, stretching up until he seemed to grow to twice his normal height, then sinking down until his head seemed to shrink into his shoulders. Then he dived into the water. He moved with the same clockwork precision: into the water, back to his log with a fish in his beak. He hit the fish smartly against the wood, first on the right, then the left: right, left, right, left. Then he tossed the fish into the air and, catching it head first, swallowed it with one gulp and looked for another straight away. He repeated the operation in quick succession until the dish was empty. A dozen fish a day, as far as our kingfisher was concerned, had been a very conservative estimate: he ate more than seventeen fish in three minutes, and finished by devouring more than one hundred in less than two days!

Feeding the kingfisher soon became the major occupation of my day. It was not the actual meal that took the time (the kingfisher saw to that efficiently enough). It was providing it.

I asked the boys who had collected the first bucketful if they could help again; at least, I intended to ask them. I went to their house and met their mother and she made it very clear that they were certainly *not* going to get me any more tiddlers; nor were they ever to go within sight or sound of that stream again. The way they had come home, and the smell of them, had been enough to frighten the cat. She could not make out why they had not both gone down with pneumonia

– only instead of pneumonia, she kept say 'poomonia'. That started St John giggling. He had to go up the road and sit behind the hedge, I found him there a few minutes later, rolling on the ground, red in the face and trying not to laugh out loud.

The keeper himself caught one pailful which lasted until midweek, and I advertised among the school children that I would pay ten pence for every ten minnows delivered. That helped until the novelty wore off. Once I loaded up the car with buckets and children, and took them out on a fishing expedition for the day, but they were much more interested in climbing trees than catching fish.

There was nothing else for it. If that kingfisher was to have fresh fish each day, I would have to catch them myself. To those of you who do not know the River Itchen, I had better tell you a bit about its geography. It looks a sleepy stream as it meanders between its gentle banks through picturesque copses – until you wade out into it and start looking for tiddlers. Then you find great potholes in the most unlikely places. One minute you will try to put your foot down on the stream bed – only to find it a foot lower than you thought, with the result that you tip head first into the water. Or a boulder might suddenly rear up in front of you and cause you to tumble head over heels. I had only taken one bucket, which was a mistake. When I did lunge out after my prey, the fish that were already in the bucket swam happily out of it. The day was not a success and, to add insult to injury, the kingfisher downed the three fish which I had managed to catch in as many seconds.

I organized things differently the next day. I took eight small boys down to the stream and gave them a jam jar each. None of them seemed a bit worried about the rain which, by the look of the clouds, had set in for the day. Rain, it seems, has an unfortunate effect on small fish: they disappear.

The boys were not perturbed. They waded straight out into the water and produced jam jar after jam jar of murky river water which they insisted were full of fish. However much I probed, I could not find anything that even remotely resembled a fish – just large amounts of mud. By this time the rain was coming down in torrents. I sent the boys back to the car and had a go myself. After a quarter of an hour, I had one little fish swimming round in my blue bucket. I passed the keeper as I ran back to the car.

He took one look at my catch and shouted out: 'It's a trout fry.' I did not stay to argue. I was so wet when we reached home that I had to cut my clothes off. They were so well moulded to my body that they seemed to have grown on to me. And, trout fry or not, that kingfisher polished off my catch in the same efficient way.

The kingfisher's stay had by now stretched into weeks. In spite of the fact that its wing was slightly dropped it seemed much better, and we hoped that, with exercise, it would regain its natural place. The trouble was that he did not exercise it if he could help it; nor did he seem to be bothered about flying. He was quite contented to remain as he was. When we tried to make him fly around in the sitting room, he simply plummeted straight to the ground and stayed there until we picked him up. He seemed happy enough, though. I do not think we have ever had a bird that has seemed so placid and contented. But what kind of a future was that for him: living with us like a piece of the furniture?

'It's no good,' John said one day. 'We've done all we can for him. He hasn't the will to fly, that's all. That's the matter with him now. If he had to fly for his food, he'd fly quickly enough. We've got to get him back to his own world so that there's the stimulus he needs to make him spread his wings.'

So the next day I descended on Charles, our gamekeeper friend. I think he wondered what had hit him. We had several ducks and geese which we had reared. They were ready to be introduced to water, and I had packed them in the back seat. The last box I took out contained the kingfisher. I explained his story to Charles and he promised to keep an eye on the bird. In addition to anything else, we had all become fond of him, and didn't want him to come to any harm.

Charles showed me a spot where the minnows always congregated and we put the kingfisher on a branch immediately above it. He bobbed his head, looked around, and seemed interested in everything that was going on. It was then that I knew he would be all right. When I called back that evening just to see if he had moved, he was still sitting on the same branch. He had not budged all day.

Charles had the answer.

'What have you been putting his food in?'

'An ordinary glass dish.'

'I reckon that's what the bird's looking for. He's become used to having his fish served up in it, and he associates food with it.'

So I went all the way home and fetched that old glass bowl. Charles waded out and put it on the river bed. The kingfisher bent down and looked at him. He was very interested in all this activity. As the disturbance in the river settled down again and the fish returned to swim in their favourite spot (right above where Charles had put the glass dish) the kingfisher changed. From where I was standing all that distance away, I could sense the change in him. He became tense and alert. Then he dived into the water and was soon back on his perch with a fish held firmly in his bill. He treated it in exactly the same way that he had treated those fish in our living room: beating it against the wood on either side of him, tossing it into the air, and swallowing it head first with one gulp. Then he dived back into the water for another, and then another ... The kingfisher had gone back to his own world.

Three years later I went back to Hampshire. The kingfishers were nesting in that part of the river for the first time in years and I wanted to see them. I wondered whether our little kingfisher would be one of the parent birds. There was no doubting where the nest burrow was: I smelt it before I saw it at the spot where the stream emptied out from the lake. As I stood there and listened to the young birds, a kingfisher launched itself across the water and flew directly towards me. I stood there without moving, hardly daring to breathe. It settled in an elder bush so close to me that I thought I could have reached out and touched it. There it sat, bobbing its head up and down in the same cheeky fashion that we had seen so often; then it was away again.

I like to think it was the bird we had helped and loved. I doubt if a truly wild bird would have flown towards me like that. But, of course, it is something I can never know for sure.

CHAPTER THREE: The Mistle Thrush

There are not many places we have not visited in this country. In the quarter of a century that we have been interested in animal rehabilitation, we have travelled to every county in England, either to collect or to release animals and birds. We prefer people to bring them to us because travelling is one of the biggest expenses we incur, but we try and help as much as we can.

Occasionally an animal or bird brings itself. A family had brought a pigeon one day. John and I walked across to their car to see them off. They sat there talking for some time, then the man started up the engine in readiness for departure. Almost immediately he turned it off again and sat there staring in front of him.

'Here's one of your birds coming home now,' he said as if he could not believe it.

We turned round and looked up the hill. A jackdaw was walking down the hill, trailing its badly broken wing. John and I looked at each other. 'It isn't one of ours. We haven't got a jackdaw with a wing in that state,' I said.

We all watched as the bird walked down the hill, and, without seeming to notice us at all, went through our gate, jumped on the doorstep and waited.

'It comes to something when your patients deliver

themselves,' the man in the car said in a tone of voice which suggested that there might be something a little peculiar about us ...

And how oddly that bird behaved! It did not struggle or object in any way when we strapped up its wing. In fact, it was an ideal patient, eating the food we gave it and not once attempting to get out of its box. It took its medicine too: the antibiotics for infection, and the calcium that we added to its diet. Birds need a lot of calcium to repair broken bones. If there is not enough in their diet, they will drain it from the healthy bones. There is nothing more depressing when one has taken a lot of care to nurse a bird that has broken a wing back to health than to see it break the other wing or a leg as soon as it is released – simply because the bone that has been mending has weakened the healthy bones by draining them of calcium.

We removed the bird's plaster on the twentieth day. It seemed to have mended well. We took it outside, opened its box, and it flew off as if it had already forgotten its three-week stay with us. We never saw it again – although I have a suspicion that it might be the very jackdaw which from time to time flies over our garden and snatches all the clothes pegs from the washing line ...

That bird certainly seemed to know where to go when it wanted help. And so did the mistle thrush. I shall never forget the day of her arrival.

It was a beautiful hot day. We were having lunch out on the lawn when a car stopped outside and a family (mother, father and two little girls) jumped out.

'I've brought you a bird,' the man said. The way in which he dropped the box at John's feet made it obvious that he was determined to leave it with us. John carefully lifted the lid and out jumped the most beautiful thrush. 'Missy', as the children came to call her, had arrived.

It hopped straight on to the table and tried to have a bath in John's cup of tea. Unfortunately, it merely succeeded in splashing every one within reach and, finally, it tipped the whole cupful in to John's lap – which made him leap up from his chair with a yell. By the time we had sorted ourselves out and St John had gone indoors to get a bowl of water for it, Missy had changed her mind about having a bath. She had found Sophie instead. She sat on her shoulder and peered right round into Sophie's face, her beak touching Sophie's nose, making sure she was having a good look. We had never experienced anything quite like this before.

'Have you hand-reared it?' John asked the man.

'It isn't a tame one, mate, it's wild.'

He could have fooled us. We looked at the bird again. It was still sitting on Sophie's shoulder, but by now it was running its beak along her hair like a bird preening its feathers.

'She ought to be wild,' the man continued. 'We reckon on how she's from the nest in the hedge down towards the village. I was doing the garden, digging it like, and she comes up the garden path squawking. So I throws her a worm and she eats that up and squawks for more. So every time I find a worm, I throws it to her like. When it gets dark, I packs up my things and goes indoors and she follows me in. She won't go out again and any way, it's dark by then. So we let her sleep on the window sill in the kitchen and I put her out when I got up next morning. When I got home from work, there she was waiting for me, and she started squawking again as soon as she saw me, calling for food she was. Well, I had to start digging afore I had my tea an' its been like that ever since – except she's moved right into the kitchen now and doesn't go out unless she has to. She seems to think I'm her Mum. She's not like it with anyone else. It's not as if I like birds. I don't object to them but they should know their proper place. This one thinks hers is in our kitchen. I've never done so much gardening in my life. You won't find a better dug garden this side of Basingstoke.'

'That's all right,' interrupted his wife, 'except we were going to leave half of it as a lawn.'

'I haven't had a chance to watch telly or go to the pub. As soon as I get home I have to start digging, and it's a job getting enough worms to satisfy her. I never knew a bird that size could eat so much. She's always hungry. We're going out for the day, so we brought him down to you.'

I have never seen anyone so relieved to get rid of anything as that man was to offload the mistle thrush. And the thrush, well, she did not mind who she was with as long as she had company.

It was the day following the one that I had taken the kingfisher to Charles and his cage was still in the lounge. I popped Missy in there until we had finished our meal. When I went in an hour later, I received the shock of my life: the thrush looked so dejected that I though it was going to die. Its head drooped; its wings hung limply down; it showed not the slightest flicker of interest in anything I said or did. Who would have believed that this was the same chirpy little bird which had tried to bathe in John's cup of tea?

'You can't keep a fit bird like that in a cage,' said John, who had just entered the room,

He opened the door of the cage, thrust his hand in, and immediately that thrush jumped in to it, fluffed up its feathers and started to look interested in life again. It flew across to my shoulder and settled down there happily, watching me do the washing up with great interest. From that time on it was my constant companion whenever I was at home. In fact, so fearless did Missy become that I had to shut her up in the cage when I went to work each day – I did not want a cat or an owl to get its claws into her. There was nothing to worry about when we were at home: she never left our side.

When I first used to put her in the cage, I would cover it with a cloth so that she could not see outside and start to pine and worry when she found she could not reach these other places. As she became used to the cage, I took the cloth away, bit by bit, until one day I did not cover it at all.

She had become as settled in her cage as she was when flying about the house after us; in fact, when the children had their friends in and they got a bit too noisy, Missy would fly into her cage by herself and stay there until things had quietened down again. It was her way of getting a bit of peace, I suppose. She would also go there if somebody whom she did not like visited the house. She had, for example, taken a great dislike to the milkman. I do not know why: he never seemed to notice her. Perhaps it was the noise he made with his bottles. Whatever the reason, whenever his van stopped outside, Missy would hop back into her cage and, peering suspiciously round the corner, refuse to come out until we heard the van start up again and grind its way up the hill. She objected to Aunt Gertrude, too, which was unfortunate: Gerty took a great interest in Missy. Being very shortsighted, she would often put her nose right into the cage in order to have a good look at her. It scared Missy stiff!

We tried to make the thrush a bit more adventuresome by encouraging her to go outside and fly around, but she would have none of it. She was perfectly happy sitting on a shoulder and joining in the conversation. Indeed, if we talked for too long and did not notice or talk to her, she would start to twitter in our ears; sometimes she would really scold us if there was something she did not like. The noises she made were piercing enough at the best of times, but when she was sitting on your shoulder, her beak almost touching your ear, the sound was enough to knock you for six!

That bird loved the children. When they ran round the garden, the thrush flew after them, getting really excited and calling out in its half-babyish voice: 'Che-cheep, che-cheep.' Sophie complained that she could not play hide and seek any more because Missy always went with her, and when she heard the other children coming nearer, she became so excited that she would call out and give the game away.

Missy seemed to prefer the noiser, running-about games. Playing with cars, reading and board games were far too quiet for her: she would tweak the children's hair and sometimes pick up one of the counters from a game and fly off with it.

We became so used to the mistle thrush, that we often forgot she was there. Several times I went shopping and did not notice the bird was still sitting on my shoulder. The first time it happened, I panicked and put up my hand to grasp hold of her so that I could carry her back to the car. The sudden movement must have startled Missy. She flew off and settled on another shopper's head. The woman started to scream as if she were being attacked by a robber rather than a harmless little thrush. It would, of course, have been better if Missy had not chosen that moment to lift her tail and make a mess all over the woman's hair. I picked the thrush up, borrowed a box from the shop and put her in that. Missy did not like it. She scolded me through the small hole which I had made in the top all the way home.

Several times she took trips with us in the car – without, I must add, having been invited. We did not see her fly into the car when we opened the door; she was so light that we did not feel her weight on our shoulder. What a shock it was when she moved or shrieked out a warning in our ears!

One day, John took her to work by mistake. We had looked everywhere for her and I was getting worried. I had to go to work and I wanted her safely in her cage before I left. She had completely disappeared. I was sure that something dreadful must have happened to her. St John and Sophie were searching out in the garden when the phone went. It was John.

'Can you come and get this perishing bird? I didn't see it fly into the car with me. I didn't even know it was on my shoulder until I walked in the office and the girls started saying: "How sweet!" Somehow I knew that they didn't mean me. What is more, it's made a mess all down the back of my decent suit.'

That was the trouble with Missy: for such a small creature, she did make a lot of mess. Some days I would be rushing off to work as usual when Sophie would say: 'Missy's been sitting on your shoulder.' I knew immediately that I would find white splashes all down my back. Missy was a very friendly bird. She would sit on anyone who called; some of them even encouraged her to sit on their shoulder. I used to feel a bit guilty when they turned round to go home and I saw that Missy had left her trade mark on them, too: the backs of their coats would be splashed white. St John often used to walk about the house with a towel draped about his shoulders like an Arab sheikh. Missy would then simply turn round the other way and make a mess down his front instead. Eventually, I had to resign myself to the extra washing.

Missy was, however, very clean in her personal habits; in fact, she was the most immaculate bird I have seen. She kept herself clean and tidy, bathing two or three times a day and preening herself constantly. She would run her beak up and down each feather four or five times before she was satisfied with it.

As it happened, when Missy came to us we were already looking after examples of the other three kinds of thrushes which are found in Britain. In fact, we had half a dozen song thrushes. They were proving a bit of a problem because they simply would not live together. When we put two of them in the same cage they fought tooth and nail until neither of them could stand.

There was only one solution: we had six thrushes and six cages. We were also looking after a smaller, slender redwing whose wing had not mended in time for it to migrate with the rest of its kind. The people who had brought it to us simply could not believe that it was a thrush at all. It seemed so much smaller than the thrushes they knew. They thought that if it was called a redwing it should have red wings too. Even when I spread out the bird's wings and showed them the bright underside, they did not seem convinced. Our two fieldfares had broken wings, too. Some people call fieldfares blue birds. When you looked at our two, you could see the reason why: their grey heads and lower parts of their backs looked blue in a certain light.

Beside these other thrushes, Missy looked huge: she was a good two inches longer than the others. From beak to tail, she measured eleven inches, and when she flew she looked bigger still. It was her size one noticed first – that, and the erect way she used to stand. She was brown with a speckled breast and two distinctive pale feathers at each side of her tail.

She seemed to know she was attractive and was always preening and tidying up her feathers. This pride in her appearance nearly caused her death once. As you know, she was very fond of a bath – the very sight of water seemed to put the idea into her head; in fact she would try and have a bath in anything liquid. People who called and were given a cup of tea or coffee seemed a bit surprised when a thrush descended on them and tried to wash in their cups. We had to keep the goldfish bowl covered, too, because she tried to wash in that. I always warned the children to put the toilet seat down: I did not want Missy having ideas about that as a suitable place to bathe. She even tried to get in the bath with Sophie one day. Depth of water and temperature did not seem to matter.

One day, I was washing up when the phone went. When I returned to the kitchen, I found Missy floating in the hot water. I thought she was dead. Her feathers were so wet that they did not look like feathers at all – more like little pieces of string. She was completely motionless. I picked her up and, much to my surprise and relief, her heart was still beating. Every part of that small body seemed to be throbbing in my hand.

Her eyes were shut and her feathers were so matted together that the pink flesh was showing.

I wrapped a towel round her and forced a single drop of brandy into her beak. She lay there so limp and pathetic that I did not think she would survive. I put her in a small box and left it near the heater in the lounge. Then I returned sadly to the washing up. About an hour later, I opened the box to see whether she was still alive. I lifted the lid and – out jumped Missy! At first she was unsteady on her feet, but that might have been the effect of the brandy. By the next morning, you would never have guessed that she had nearly drowned the day before. She flew around the room as happily and chirpily as ever.

Sometimes I thought that Missy had a charmed life. She once tried to drive the neighbour's cat out of the garden. It responded by lashing out and snatching her up by the wing. Fortunately, our dog cannot stand cats: he chased it up the nearest tree and, on the way, it dropped the mistle thrush. He set up such a noise that we dashed out to see what was the matter. When we found Missy, she was helplessly flapping her wings, she could not raise herself more than a couple of inches from the ground. The cat had pulled all the primary feathers from one wing and left her flightless. Missy was housebound for ten days until her new feathers grew. She did not like that at all: she would sit on the window sill watching the children playing in the garden, and looking really sorry for herself. When they came in she would fly across and scold them as if it was their fault that she was stuck indoors.

Then one day Missy was gone. She had been with us for eleven months, living as one of the family. I doubt if anyone can realize how much we missed that small bird; how much a part of our lives she had become. She had been changing since March when the thrushes and blackbirds in the garden had begun to pair. She spent less and less time pursuing the children. We would find her more and more often perched in the overgrown hedge at the other side of the paddock. We always knew exactly where she was because she made far more noise than any of the other birds and nearly always came back to the cottage with us to sit on one of our shoulders.

Then one morning she flew out of the kitchen window and we never saw her again. We spent hours searching for her. There were plenty of mistle thrushes about, but none that came when we called them. The following winter we had a small flock of mistle thrushes living in the paddock. Was Missy one of them? We never knew for sure.

CHAPTER FOUR: The Grass Snake

Why do so many people look as though they would like to run a mile when they see a snake? I cannot say that they are the sort of creature I would go out and look for. All the same, I like to know about them – the same as I do about all sorts of wild life. What is more, snakes have as much right to live on this earth as we do. St John, on the other hand, has always been fascinated by snakes, and he generally keeps one or two around the house. The trouble is that we dare not even mention the word snake when Mrs Bellamy comes to see us. She cannot stand them!

There is rather a lot of Mrs Bellamy. She is a happy, round sort of person. Sophie says her shape reminds her of a cottage loaf. She helps us with the housework. Because we could not manage without her, we make doubly sure that St John's snakes are well and truly out of her way when we know that a visit is due.

All the same, we came home one day to find Mrs Bellamy in a dreadful state. We wondered what the noise was when we opened the door. Rushing into the hall, we found that she had balanced the kitchen stool on the stairs and was perched on it. She was shivering so violently that her teeth were chattering. She had been cleaning the stairs when a snake had slithered between her legs . . .

We simply did not know how that particular

creature had escaped from the aquarium – until, that is, St John found a small hole in the side of the lid. It was so small that we did not think there was a chance of the snake getting through it – but it had. We put it back into the aquarium and watched as it effortlessly slithered its way out again. Snakes move beautifully: they stretch and flow, stretch and flow so smoothly.

That snake had stretched and flowed through that minute hole with no difficulty at all. It could extend itself until it was only a quarter of its normal width – just like a piece of elastic.

This is, of course, one of the reasons why it is so difficult to keep snakes. They seem to have an inbuilt ability to be where they want to be. They can squeeze through the tiniest of holes. I remember one particular incident very clearly. A man who had suffered an accident was rushed to hospital, and his snakes, which he kept in his cellar, had escaped. No one knew how many snakes there were, or whether they were dangerous. We arrived just in time to see one of them disappear through a hole so narrow that even a spider on a diet would have had difficulty getting through. The gap (it could not have been more than half an inch wide) was where the pipes passed underneath the houses. And we had seen what looked like a half grown python disappearing down it! The police had to evacuate the whole row of houses: all the cellars were adjacent to each other and it was impossible to say at which house this snake (or these snakes!) was going to surface. Fortunately, it all ended well. The man was not badly hurt. By the time he came home, the snake had returned of its volition to its favourite hunting ground – which the owner pointed out to us. The snake was curled around the lamp shade above our heads. We had been in that room many times and had not seen it return. Snakes are, of course, so quiet, and move about so smoothly and silently that some people regard them as sinister creatures and, consequently, mistrust them.

It was lunchtime when we received the phone call. The local police were on the line. The policeman described a snake in great detail, and then asked me whether I could identify it. It sounded like a grass snake. Could I confirm that it was not dangerous in any way? I said that I would not like to confirm one way or the other without having seen it. He then asked me whether I could put him in touch with a snake expert.

'St John's here,' I replied.

'He'll do,' the policeman said. 'Could you get him up here quickly? It's an emergency.'

The village was not far away but, as I drove there, St John started to take all his clothes off.

'Whatever are you doing?' I asked in amazement.

'Well, it's sure to be a grass snake,' he said. 'They always are. I expect they'll want us to move it, and if you so much as touch a wild grass snake, it ejects a stinking liquid. I don't want to be covered with it. You can't wash it off. It has to wear off and that takes weeks.'

The police van was waiting for us. The policeman pointed to the place where he had last seen the snake, and then jumped into his van, shut the door and wound up the window. We had never seen anything like it: the village is usually a very busy place, with people gossiping in the streets and children playing on the green. That day, there was not another human being in sight; every door and window was tightly shut.

The snake was nowhere to be seen either.

We were standing in front of a big old house surrounded by lawns. Close to the front door a gnarled old tree was growing; dead leaves were heaped up round the base of its trunk, and we caught sight of a hole which went down towards the roots. If there was a snake, that was just the kind of home it would choose. Had I not, I wondered, seen a slither of movement when we got out of the car? I searched around. Faces were pressed against window panes the whole length of the road. I have never felt so conspicuous in my life! Suddenly, I made up my mind: there was only one thing for it. I lay on my stomach, reached into the hole, felt something long and cool and pulling it out quickly, tossed whatever I had grasped towards St John. St John put out his hands and, without thinking, caught the snake. The snake reacted by secreting its evil-smelling liquid down his chest and one arm. St John tried to catch the rest of the liquid which the snake was discharging in the jar I had brought. Holding the snake in one hand, he then screwed on the lid of the jar with the other.

'I thought we'd put the snake in the jar to get it home,' I said.

'But I've caught the liquid in that and I want to keep it.'

I knocked on the door of the house, but the woman would not answer it. Moments later, she came to the window.

'Have you a spare plastic bag?' I shouted. 'I want to put the snake in it.' I had to shout my request half a dozen times before she understood what I wanted. Even then she would not open the door – despite the fact that St John had firm hold of the reptile. She opened the letter box and pushed the bag out to me, a little bit at a time.

It was a common grass snake. Why, when people see any creature which resembles a snake do they automatically assume that it's an adder, and that an adder's only aim in life is to bite them? Adders are quiet, retiring animals which only bite when they are suddenly disturbed or threatened.

Our grass snake, which was a good three feet in length, was a real beauty. Its size alone ought to have suggested that it was not an adder, which rarely grows to more than two feet. I have seen the skin of one in the Natural History Museum which was twenty-eight inches long – but that was unusual. This snake was greeny-brown in colour; the black markings on its underside made it look much darker. Its brown eyes seemed especially large for a snake. Behind its head were two yellow patches which almost joined in the centre of its back, and made it look as though it was wearing a collar.

As St John stood there, jam jar in one hand and snake in the other, it began to hiss and twist about as though it were trying to whip the hand that held it. I opened the plastic bag. It slid inside and curled itself into a small, twisted, angry knot. Would anyone who saw it like that have believed that it could have stretched out to three feet? I doubt it.

I took the bag across to the policeman and pointing to it, informed him that it was indeed a grass snake. I asked him what he would like us to do with it.

'I'd like it taken as far away as possible,' he said firmly.

'It won't hurt anyone. It's quite harmless,' I replied.

But the policeman was not interested. He simply

did not want to know. We got in the car and took it home. As we drove along, I said to St John: 'I reckon there was another one down that hole.'

'Two or three more,' he confided. 'It's just the sort of place they would go to at this time of the year. It's ideal for hibernation. In spite of the fact that it's only September, the weather's been pretty chilly. They will have started to gather in spots like that in readiness for the winter.'

We had lunch when we got home. I said I would take the snake down to the copse that afternoon and let it go. As so often happens, things did not work out as planned. A group of women came down from the village while we were still eating and said that they had heard we were releasing snakes in the area. They did not like the idea at all. I explained that it was only a single, harmless grass snake. I fetched the bag from the car and St John lifted it out to show them. They were absolutely horrified. Over the years, we have released badgers, buzzards, all sorts of different animals from the centre. Yet as soon as we thought about putting out a snake, no matter how harmless, we had the village people descending on us. St John tried to explain that it was only humane to take it out into the woods. Seeing the genuine anxiety on their faces, however, I promised that we would not release it locally.

Fortunately St John had a snake pit in the garden that year. Later that afternoon, we took it out and popped the snake into it. I spent the rest of the day digging the garden for worms. I need not have bothered: it refused to eat; in fact it did not settle down at all. It would move round and round that pit, hissing and darting its tongue in and out. Then it would curl up on the surface and become quiet. That was a most unusual reaction. Normally snakes try and get out of sight – beneath a stone or down a hole. This one simply lay there. I told St John that I would take it across to Stapleford Woods in the morning and let it go there.

As it happened, we had another call the following morning. A big red deer stag had found its way into someone's garden and had entangled itself in the clothes line. I spent the whole morning trying to release it.

When I got home, I found St John staring into his snake pit with fascination. 'Come and look at this,' he shouted. I went across, still feeling a bit washed out from the exertions of the morning: that stag had been one of the most difficult animals I had ever tried to help. As soon as I reached the pit, I forgot my tiredness. The grass snake was giving out a row of what looked like small oblong, plastic bags. It was laying eggs. They were all connected to each other, and came out in a long, knotted string. She went on and on and on, sometimes stopping and resting for a while before starting again. Once the eggs were laid, they seemed to start growing – like bubbles. St John explained that the eggs were absorbing the moisture from the air.

It was evening before she had laid the last one. When she had finished, she curled up on the opposite side of the box as if they were nothing to do with her. She was simply not interested in them. St John counted thirty-eight eggs altogether. He was worried because they were so late.

'They generally lay their eggs much earlier in the year. These will hardly have hatched before it's time for them to hibernate.'

I suggested that I take the snake and its eggs to

Stapleford Woods the following morning. St John had a better idea. He collected the eggs and took them across the fields to where the farmer had a pile of manure. He buried them in it. 'The warmth will encourage them to hatch more quickly,' he said.

The next two days were so busy that it was not until three days later that I found the time to take the snake to the woods. When I went to fetch it, it was not there. We emptied out the whole pit, but there was no grass snake in it. Only its skin had been left as a memento. It had sloughed its whole skin like a vest that does not fit it any more, leaving the whole thing unbroken and inside out. Not one of the scales had been disturbed; even the transparent skin over the lens of the eye had been discarded with the rest.

We never did understand how that snake escaped: the sides of the pit were two feet high. I think that it may have slithered up one of the tufts of long grass which grew in the centre, and reached the edge in that way.

A week later, one of the tractor drivers called out that our snake was in the stack yard. When we arrived, we found not one but two grass snakes. One of them could have been ours. The farmer said he could not remember when he had last seen grass snakes on the farm. But he was not worried about them; in fact, he seemed to welcome their presence. We left them undisturbed.

The following summer, we found three small grass snakes in the field near the manure heap. None of them was a foot long. Had those eggs hatched out successfully after all?

CHAPTER FIVE: The Fox

It is not only snakes that arouse emotions in people, and make them feel apprehensive: I think that of all the British creatures which have this effect, the fox must head the list. There is undoubtedly something very attractive about a fox: it is such a proud, alert creature that the mere sight of one can often give people a lot of pleasure. Somehow a fox seems to embody the very spirit of the countryside. Yet the animal still seems to arouse a certain wariness in people. Can such an attractive animal *really* be such a ruthless killer? There are other country dwellers who have witnessed the damage done by these animals, and who consequently hate the very sight of them. It always amazes me that a wild animal can create such violent feelings in a human being. And then there are those people who are genuinely worried by the diseases which wild animals, and foxes in particular, can carry. It is already known that on the continent they carry rabies, one of the most dreaded diseases in the world.

When a fox is brought to us, our feelings are different altogether. We carefully consider whether it is going to adapt to living at the centre; we wonder what our chances are of returning it to the wild.

It is not that there is any trouble in persuading a fox to go wild. At one time, indeed, we doubted whether there was really such a thing as a tame fox. I am still in two minds. However tame it may seem, if a fox has complete freedom of movement at all times, sooner or later its wild instincts will be aroused again, and it will be called back to its own world. It may be the presence of another fox; the scent of a hare; the mating instinct. Whatever the stimulus, once it feels the call of the wild, it responds immediately. One minute a contented fox is running round the yard; the next it has gone. It takes approximately nine months to rehabilitate a badger; a fox adapts to the wild again in the same number of days.

So much of a fox's behaviour is instinctive: it has a basic animal cunning, for example, which is so highly developed that it is often mistaken for intelligence. It kills by instinct. Even if it is not hungry, it will pounce and kill anything that is smaller or weaker than itself. If you ever see a hen house or a pheasant coop after a fox has been through it, it is a sight which you never forget. This instinct begins to develop as soon as the cub is born. I have seen an eleven-week-old fox cub take a fully grown Rhode Island hen.

It is small wonder, then, that landowners resent our releasing foxes on their property. We are particularly careful not to release them on land which is hunted. We knew one woman who, after rearing a fox cub, let it go one day by leaving it in the countryside. When the hunt came through that area, the fox, who had become used to dogs when it had been in captivity, ran up to the hounds and was torn to pieces. I would hate that to happen to any animal which had been in my care. In recent years, farmers have allowed us to release the odd dog fox on their land. Vixens, however, are another matter altogether: farmers do not want their land to be overrun with the creatures.

Many rats have become immune to warfarin: they can eat the poison without it affecting them. But they are no match for the fox. There is nothing quite like a fox for keeping rats under control. Watching foxes hunt rats is an hypnotic sight: as you gaze at the two predators, a drama unfolds in which cunning matches cunning and instinct matches instinct. The fox, however, wins every time: the final pounce is always deadly and decisive.

However safe we make our runs, we always worry when we have a fox at the centre. Will it escape and attack the other birds and animals? We never keep a fox in a pen unless it has a double door; we always ensure that a double layer of wire has been laid on the ground. Even if they seem to accept captivity for the time, they will often simply be waiting for their chance to escape. They do not react like other wild animals: pacing up and down, completely frustrated by confinement in a small space. It is their habit to sit and watch everything which is going on with great interest. But if you leave one of the doors open or fail to notice a piece of wire that has come undone, the fox will be out.

One day last summer, St John went in to water a fox which had a broken leg. Fortunately. the leg was still in plaster, which slowed the fox down a bit. St John had not shut the first door properly. Between opening the second door, and bending down to pick up the bucket, that fox had escaped. Before St John had time to realize what had happened, the fox had a stray cat in one bite and was making a bee line for Sophie's rabbit. John, who was on the lawn at the time, saw what had happened, and made a dive for the fox. Before he had hold of him properly, it had twisted round and savaged him. We recaptured the creature, but spent the rest of the night with John at the hospital.

In the past, certain foxes seem to have appreciated that we were trying to help them. They have been as amenable as that one was vicious. One fox in particular I will always remember. A small car stopped outside our gate one afternoon. It was parked there a long time and I went out to see what the people wanted. As soon as they realized that they had reached the right house they began to pour out of the car: Mum, Dad and the four children. That was not all, either: they had left Grandma and a huge packing case on the back seat. I would not like to say which was the more difficult to get out. How they got either of them in I will never know. Grandma, however, helped with the box: she just sat on the back seat and pushed. The box was half in and half out when it jammed, and it was not until all four children had climbed into the back of the car with Grandma and they had all begun to push at the same time, that the box popped out like the cork from a champagne bottle. The man and I were left sitting in the middle of the road holding the box between us.

'It's a fox,' he said with a smile as we sat there.

Whatever it was, I imagined that it would be badly shaken up by its recent experience. I eased open the top of the box and looked at the animal inside. She stared back at me with her soft brown eyes, not one bit perturbed.

'It just turned up,' the man said casually. 'The wife put the food out for the cat and this here fox walks up the garden path and starts drinking the milk. Then it ate the meat. But I think there's something wrong with it because it doesn't seem able to swallow properly and it was sick. Then it curled up on the back step and went to sleep. The old cat wouldn't come past it. She's disappeared. We haven't seen her since last night. When I want out to empty the tea-pot this morning, the fox was still there. It just opened one eye, looked at me, and went back to sleep again. So we've brought it up here.'

I knew straight away where the fox had come from. We had been called down to a house not far from the village where this family lived. This person had had a fox problem, too. We knew Pauline well. Being a lover of animals of all kinds, she had kept a pet fox which had the run of the house and garden. One day she had gone out to call her fox in and, to her amazement, not one but two foxes stared back at her. They looked so alike that for a little while she did not know which was which. She had given the new fox food. It had eaten hungrily, and promptly been sick. She had phoned us up and asked whether we would go down and collect it. We told her to see if it was still around the next day. She phoned later on to say that it had disappeared as silently as it had arrived. It had obviously moved in with our family further down the road.

As luck would have it, I had an empty run – well . . . a half-empty run anyway. I had kept a badger in it for some time. We used to let the badger out each night, and it only came home now if it remembered. Sometimes we were woken up at about four o'clock in the morning by an angry badger banging his food dish on the ground, demanding that it be filled immediately; sometimes we would not see him for days on end. If he had decided to come home that night, it would have been hard luck. We managed to squeeze the box through the door and into the run. I opened it up so that the fox could move round if she wanted. To our surprise, she seemed quite happy to lie there on the straw and gaze up at us with interest. I made quite sure that the door was firmly shut before I showed the family some of the other birds and animals which we were caring for at that time. Matters were complicated by the fact that Grandma wanted to poke everything with her umbrella – just to make sure that they were still alive. I wondered what she was doing with an umbrella in the first place: it was a scorching hot mid-summer's day. Perhaps she thought it would protect her. She seemed to be frightened of anything that moved, and jumped right up in the air when a tawny owl leaned forward and hooted in her face. She told me repeatedly how much she disliked animals. If that was the case, how had the rest of the family persuaded her to travel in the back seat with that fox? That is a mystery I never resolved.

An old swan saved the day. She took a violent dislike to the youngest child, chasing him menacingly up the path, her wings outstretched and hissing all the time. That finished Grandma. She could not get back into the car fast enough.

When the family had gone, I took some warm milk and glucose out to the fox. She drank it down as if she had not seen food for days. As soon as she had finished eating she began to retch – and then threw a fit. It was then that I caught sight of her hind legs: they were red raw. The fur from tail to toes looked as if it had been pulled away; her flesh was open and sore.

John came home from work as I was examining her. Normally he has only one priority when he gets in: the tea pot. That day he did not even wait to change his clothes. He bundled the fox back into the box and took it straight to the vet's in Lincoln.

'I doubt if Colin will be able to save it, and let us

keep it alive,' he said. 'It's in a dreadful state.'

He was wrong. Colin took one look at it and said: 'I know what's happened to this creature. Two dogs have been brought in this week, and they were both in this state. Weedkiller's the problem: it collects in small puddles after spraying, and doesn't sink into the ground. These animals sit in it. Look: it's been burned. Do you know what happens then? In trying to clean themselves up, they lick the infected places and transfer the stuff to their mouths and throats.'

He opened the fox's mouth and showed us the animal's throat: as far down as we could see it was covered with blisters.

'That's why it's been sick so often. It will survive; but the burns will take at least three weeks to heal. You'll have to keep it on a milk diet until that throat's cleared up, and it *must* take these tablets three times a day. Keep the raw parts covered with this cream.'

Three times a day we had to rub the fox's bottom with thick white cream that seemed to get everywhere except the right place. As the animal regained his strength, he began to wriggle and struggle as soon as we began to smear on the cream. John often used to come into breakfast each morning with white cream all over his hair; his shoes and clothes would also be covered in the stuff. Somehow he always seemed to collect a particularly large splodge on the end of his nose. It smelt a bit strong, too: St John and Sophie used to sit and giggle when father came in and that made him cross. In the end when they saw him coming in from the fox each morning, they used to pick up their breakfasts and run – but we could always hear them giggling upstairs.

The pills posed a similar problem. The fox readily

accepted them in the first few days. Unfortunately, when she grew stronger she decided they were not for her. She would hold one in her mouth until she thought we were no longer looking, and would then deposit it in a corner of the run. It used to make John so angry. He would march back up to her and push it down her throat again. Five minutes later, it would re-appear. This went on half a dozen times each morning until the thing finally disappeared. We always hoped it had gone where it was meant to. When she began to get better and we added minced chicken to her diet, we would hide a pill in the meat. When she had finished, the plate would be as clean as if it had been polished – except for one small, white pill which would be sitting in the middle of it.

At first, the fox had found it difficult to even lap, and we had had to feed her with a medicine dropper. That period only lasted for a day or two. As soon as she was lapping we added calcium and Complan to the liquid. She did not mind what we gave her; she ate it all: except that pill.

She began to object to captivity, too, now that she was getting better; but she had to put up with it until she was quite fit. In spite of the fact that the fox's health was improving, its fits did not stop; in fact, they became longer and more violent and were frightening to watch. We knew from experience, however, that these fits were her way of reacting to captivity. This is the trouble with a really wild animal like a fox: it cannot tolerate confinement. All we could do was to keep it quiet and undisturbed until its throat had healed enough for it to swallow. The vet took all kinds of tests to make sure that there was no medical reason for the fits and as soon as he reassured us on this point we hastened to get that animal fit enough to return to its own world.

It was Sophie who noticed that the animal never threw fits when there were only the four of us around; whenever someone came to the door or a stray dog put its nose through the gate, however, the fox would throw a violent fit. As soon as we had discovered this fact, we moved the run right back, and made a rule that no one was to be allowed near her.

At first we had kept her in the stable. It is an old stone-floored building which dates from the days when the cottage was used as a post house. Huge rafters span the roof. As soon as the fox had begun to associate John's appearance in the stable with bottom rubbing and pill pushing, she would run up the wall along the rafters, and dodge round and behind him. It would take him twenty times longer to catch her than to give her the dose, and he declared that if these antics did not give the fox a heart attack, it would give him one. So we put her back in the small run, simply because we could catch her more easily, and make sure that she was taking the medicine she needed.

Sophie had been quite right: the fox accepted the four of us with no qualms, and now that we were keeping her in a quieter place, she rarely threw a fit. Troubles of a different sort cropped up then. Why, when you ask people to keep away from something, do they make a bee line for it as soon as your back is turned? It is always the same. If we are looking after a nervous bird like a heron and ask people not to go near the spot where it is being kept, nine times out of ten you will hear them calling their children to come and see it, or they will have decided that they must have a photograph. Similarly, as soon as we asked callers to keep away from the fox, they would immediately want to go and see what they had to keep away from.

Two men in particular were very difficult. They were supposed to be biologists so they should have known better. It was not only that they went and looked at the fox when we asked them to keep away: as soon as our backs were turned, they would be leaning over the run, gazing down at her. Their behaviour nearly drove the animal mad. Each time they went towards it, she threw another fit. Even when John shouted at them, they would not leave her alone. We had not invited either of them. They had arrived with the attitude that they were entitled to nose around because they worked for a charity. Looking back now, we should have called the police straight away; but all we knew then was that we had to contend with two men who had invited themselves into our home, and who obviously had no respect for us, our work with the animals or the animals themselves.

We learned the hard way, unfortunately: this experience left the fox almost as sick as she had been in at the beginning, and we had to coax her to accept the pills all over again.

It was nearly three months after her arrival that Sophie and I moved the fox down to the release pens. When we took her out of the box and put her in the large, straw-filled stable, you would never have dreamed she had been so ill. She looked magnificent: her alert brown eyes watched us warily; her small, pointed ears turned first this way and then that, moving independently of each other to catch the different sounds.

We fed her only on rats and rabbits now: this was

what the landowner wanted her to catch. On the third night the door was left open, but the food was still put out for her. She would often pad to the doorway and gaze at the outside world. But it was another three weeks before she ventured out herself – and then she ran back at the slightest sound of an unfamiliar noise. Gradually she became more confident, and started catching her own food – mainly rats. We attached an ear tag before she was released so that she could be easily identified.

She is still in the woods where we let her go, and is now a completely wild animal once more. From the minute she was given her freedom, she never threw another fit; in fact it would now be impossible to know her from any of the other wild foxes were it not for one thing: her insatiable interest in people. She will sit in the hedgerow and watch any human being who passes with the greatest curiosity. People seem to fascinate her.

CHAPTER SIX: The Manx Shearwater

Can there be any instance in this world when clumsiness is replaced by such immediate beauty, where helplessness becomes such instant power and strength as when the shearwater takes to the air?

Shearwaters are wonderful birds. They have such extraordinary powers of flight that I have whiled away hours watching them. You see immediately how they have earned their name: they skim in the shallow thermals of air between the waves, lifting over the crests and letting the currents in the troughs carry them forward. Occasionally, they will use their wings to gain momentum before they are off again, carried by the natural movement of the air. They fly so close to the waves that at times it seems as if they really are shearing the water. Their smooth, gliding, powerful flight has a completely hypnotic effect on me. They twist and turn in the air with such dexterity that one second you can see their dark plumage and, the next, you catch a glimpse of their white underparts. When they are flying together and their movements are caught by the rays of the sun, they have the appearance of crinkling silver paper.

It is not often that I see a bird whose beauty and grace completely takes my breath away: a shearwater in flight is one of the few. They are birds of the ocean. Not only do they possess grace, power and beauty in the air, but they have remarkable staying powers: when nesting off the west coast of Britain, they will think nothing of flying for their daily food to the Bay of Biscay. Manx shearwaters which have been ringed off the English coast have later been found in Australia and West Africa.

To me, a shearwater represents everything which is noble in a bird: power, beauty of movement, freedom and complete dominance of its own environment.

Yet on land they are helpless. Their legs grow near the back of their bodies. It is consequently impossible for them to balance: when they try to stand up, they simply tip forward. At best they can shuffle round on the ground. You will only see shearwaters on the land at night time. By day, they are at sea or in their nesting holes. They nest in burrows under the ground, rather like a rabbit's. They shuffle from them in the most ungainly way at dusk, and the air is filled with their weird, long drawn out cries which send shivers down your back and make the whole place feel eerie. Some country people call them ghost birds and you only have to hear them once to know how they earned that name. I am sure that some of the old tales of smugglers' ghosts which walked at midnight were really shearwaters calling.

Because shearwaters are so helpless on the land they provide easy victims for the black-backed gulls which prey on them mercilessly. The slaughter on a clear, moonlit night is horrific; the earth around the mouths of their burrows is littered with corpses. Buzzards, too, fly in for the killing, their dark silhouettes look menacing in the fading light. I realize that this is how nature works, but I hate to see it. Yet I watch it time after time, almost hypnotized by the whole procedure, feeling completely helpless in the face of such final menacing powers; knowing that this is life as it is lived in the wild and that I have no chance of intruding or influencing it in any way. If I do chase off some of the predators, they will only find other victims or return to take the others when I am not there to protect them. It is usually only a short distance from a burrow to the edge of the cliff, and once they have shuffled those few metres forward, they can launch themselves into the air and immediately they become all-powerful fearing attack from no living thing.

There are eight different species of shearwater but the one which is found on the British coast is the Manx variety. Knowing that they are found at sea, we are always a little surprised when one of them is brought to the centre, yet in the past twenty years, we have had seventy-three.

Sophie and I were tramping over the fields when the most recent one arrived. It was a beautiful autumnal evening. The russet colours of September were beginning to overtake the bright greens of summer. The willows along the stream were yellowing; the elder flashed pink in the hedgerows. The sun's evening rays caught and emphasized the colours; our arms tingled with the warmth. The weather seemed to be making amends for the three days of continuous wind and rain which we had just had.

We had gone out to collect mushrooms. The fields beneath our village still show the patterns of ridges and furrows of mediaeval farming. Rain collects in the dips; the grass becomes patterned with mushrooms. We had not picked one before Sophie said, 'There's a car outside.'

Hough on the Hill is a small village on the Lincoln

Cliff. The cottages cluster up the hillside and are dominated by the Norman tower of the Church which stands sentinel above the village and can be seen from miles around. Our house is the last one, the big red-brick square house that is half way down the hill.

In spite of the fact that we were nearly two miles across the fields, we could look back and see clearly what was going on.

'St John's there,' I replied. 'He can see what they want.'

'Mum, there's another car there.'

'Leave it to St John.'

'I expect it's another bird,' Sophie said as she put the first mushrooms into her basket.

When we got back, not one bird had been brought in, but three. A little owl had been knocked over by a car. It did not seem too badly hurt. The car had hit it on the head, causing slight concussion. St John had settled that one down in a cardboard box. The second bird was proving a bit of a problem. It was a heron with a badly broken wing – so badly broken that the bone was protruding through the skin and I knew we would have to get to the vet's quickly. It had lost a lot of blood, too. One look at the floor made that clear. St John had tried to put it in a box but we did not have one tall enough. As soon as it had been put away, it simply lifted one leg up, wound its long thin toes over the rim and eased itself up, over and out.

St John was pleased to see us back. He was a bit concerned about the heron; it was not only the wing which worried him but the bird itself. Herons are odd creatures to handle: one moment they seem calm and settled, the next they will suddenly stab out with those dagger-like beaks. I slid my fingers over this bird's neck to feel the position of its head, and then examined it carefully. The wing looked bad and the bird itself was in poor condition. It was very, very thin: I did not think it had much of a chance.

The third bird was a Manx shearwater. The people who had brought it were still there, holding it in their arms. I did not have time to say much to them, or even to think how strange it was to find someone standing in a kitchen in the middle of England cradling a shearwater. I had a quick look at it. In spite of the fact that it was very thin and breathing heavily, it did not seem injured. I settled it in a box and asked the people if they would like to come back later. The heron had to be seen by the vet before we did anything else.

It was nearly midnight before I had a chance of looking once more at the shearwater. It seemed a drab, dull little bird at first glance: nearly fifteen inches long, the feathers were dull and black. They lacked the glossy appearance of gull's feathers or the kittiwake's. Its breast was white. Its dark beak was topped by the two round nasal tubes that you find on all petrels and which give them such a comical appearance. The bird sat there passively: it did not seem to be interested in anyone or anything; neither, on the other hand, did it object to being handled. It seemed quite happy to be with us, and looked round with its small, bright eyes.

Seeing that bird sitting there reminded me of the first shearwaters we had ever helped. On that occasion, they were not brought to us: we found them ourselves (at least, John did) in the middle of a car park.

The children were smaller then and we had gone down to Pembroke for a holiday. We were staying in a caravan near the coast. It was the only kind of holiday we could have: we had had to take about twenty sick birds along with us. It had been a long journey down and it was dark when we arrived. John decided he would take the dog for a walk while we got ourselves to bed. I had just got into bed myself when there was a violent knocking at the door. I nearly jumped out of my skin. I opened the door a crack and John thrust a bird into my hands with the words: 'Quick, there's some more down there,' and ran off again before I had a chance to reply. I was left there holding the bird; I had no idea what it was. I did not immediately associate the chubby little bird in my hand with the long-winged, powerful shearwaters which I so loved to watch. I thought it might be a shearwater because of its nasal tubes, but I was not sure. Before I could look them up in my bird book, John was back at the door. This time he thrust two of them into my hands before he disappeared again. It was on his fifth journey that I tentatively suggested that perhaps they should be there anyway.

'I don't think so,' John said. 'It doesn't seem right. They can't get up into the air. They're shuffling round all over the place. There's a couple of stray dogs roaming round, too. I thinks it's best if we keep them here tonight and take them back to the sea in the morning.'

I found them in the bird book: they were definitely Manx shearwaters. By the time I persuaded John to come to bed, we had eighteen of them. What with those, the six guillemots which we were planning to release while on holiday, the two tawny owls and all our other patients, there was not an inch of space left. We had to be careful where we put our feet.

The shearwaters did not seem to be any trouble: they gazed placidly up from the ground, and showed no interest whatsoever in the food and drink which we offered them. The trouble didn't start until about two o'clock in the morning.

I woke up with a start. Whatever could be happening? There was such a dreadful noise that I thought someone was being murdered. I sat up in bed and fumbled for the torch, catching hold of everything else in my haste, including John's ear. He sat up with a shout; Sophie called out that she was frightened. By the time we had sorted ourselves out, there was not a sound to be heard: everywhere was absolutely quiet.

John snatched the torch and stumbled out in his pyjamas. He looked under the car and shone the light on the caravan: everything seemed normal. So we all settled down to go to sleep again. Ten minutes later the noise started again, a long, drawn-out wail that sent a shiver down my spine.

I shook John awake. He had dropped off to sleep again as soon as his head touched the pillow. 'Listen,' I hissed. There it was again: a long drawn-out wail, high-pitched and eerie. As that cry died away, another, and then another, filled the air until the whole caravan was reverberating with the gathering crescendo of sound. John reached for the torch again. As soon as there was any movement, the noise stopped: silence reigned once more.

'It's the shearwaters,' John whispered. 'They must be hungry.'

So we sat up in bed and forced mashed-up sprats down their throats. It would have been easier if the birds themselves had been a bit more helpful. They simply waited until we had eased the food into their beaks and then shuffled backwards, shaking their heads and spraying us with the food. It was surprising how far the pieces of mashed-up fish were scattered. However often I scrubbed that caravan, I did not seem to get rid of the fishy smell. At last we had made sure they all had something in their stomachs. Settling them back in their boxes, we went back to sleep ourselves. At least, that was the idea; however, the minute the lights went out, the chorus started up again. That was too much for John. He bundled the birds out to the car. Then the four of us buried our heads under the bed clothes and let the shearwaters 'sing' to their hearts' content. The next morning, the people in the next caravan asked us if we had heard a funny noise in the night. We pretended that we did not know what they were talking about.

The mists had cleared during the night, blown away by the strong winds.

As soon as we had finished our breakfast, we took the shearwaters back to the sea. We felt tired as we walked down the road, but however much those birds had disturbed us in the night, we were pleased that we had found them. We passed the corpses of several other shearwaters on the road, ones like ours which must have landed and, having been unable to launch themselves into the air again, had been run over by cars.

We had ten birds in a wicker work-basket and another eight in two large boxes which we managed to carry between us, St John and Sophie trundled along behind. St John was carrying the movie camera: we were determined to get some film of these birds as they went back to the sea. We told him where to stand and which shots he should take. It is a great pity that we never seem to have time to take the notes or photographs that we would like. That day, however, we were organised: or so we thought. We had planned exactly how we were going to take them out of the boxes and put them into the sea; as often happens, things did not quite work out as planned.

John opened the hamper, bent down to pick up the first bird and the whole thing exploded in his face. There were shearwaters everywhere, all travelling in the wrong direction. Not one of those birds headed for the sea; they all started shuffling back the way we had come. It was surprising the speed they could work up once they got going. John moved into action straight away, dashing round the beach in a vain attempt to head them off and guide them back to the water. I had been showing St John how to wind the camera; I stood there with the thing in my hand, startled by the sudden burst of activity. It is enough to say that we did not take the film as planned. Instead, I have some fine film of alternating sky, sea and sand, with a short appearance of John haring across the screen. He is not the most athletic person at the best of times, but he did manage to catch up with one of those shearwaters and thrust it into my hands.

'Get it back into the sea,' he gasped.

I dutifully took the bird from him and waded out into the water until it reached my knees. I placed the bird back in the sea, whereupon it promptly nose-dived and buried its beak firmly in the sand. I had to dive after it and try to get it to float again, all the time going out deeper and deeper. I was nearly up to my neck before I finally persuaded that bird to remain horizontal.

By the time I returned to the basket, John had caught two more birds. These proved just as difficult as the first. They seemed keener to get out than stay in the water. As I coaxed them out to deeper water, the children ran up and down the tide line waving their hands and shouting in order to discourage them from heading back towards the beach. Only one of them seemed happy to be reintroduced to the water. As we watched, it lifted into the air and flew off over the horizon. We had earlier decided that it was the only adult bird: all the others were young ones. I do not know why it took them such a long time to accept the sea again. We could only assume that their experiences in the caravan had completely disorientated them. Eventually, however, they were all swimming just beneath the surface of the water with a fluency of movement that was beautiful to watch, surfacing every so often as they swam further and further out from the shore.

By now we were absolutely exhausted. It had taken us three hours to persuade those birds to go. We sank on to the sand and watched them as they gathered in a small colony about a quarter of a mile out, bobbing gently on the waves.

We slowly gathered ourselves together. I was soaked. My clothes clung to me as if they were my skin; the others were not much better. It was then that we realized for the first time that we had an audience. When we had gone down to the beach it had been completely deserted except for a couple of stray dogs; now there were two or three hundred people gathered by the steps that led up to the road.

Two round-faced men were sitting on the sand, tears streaming down their faces. A Welshman came up and shook John by the hand, remarking that he had never seen such a funny sight in his life. When we walked through the crowd on our way back to the caravan, they began to clap as if we had put on a free show for their benefit.

There were two results of that episode: one was that we were offered a boat, which meant that we could take the birds further out from the beach and release them in deeper water; secondly, many visitors to the area had discovered where we were staying, with the result we were brought a steady supply of injured birds.

We had to erect a couple of temporary cages beside the caravan: it became a real home from home. Among the injured were several more Manx shearwaters. One of them had been picked up on a road twenty miles inland; another had been found on top of a hedge. All that was required was to return them to the sea. What surprised us was the fact that it took those birds between three days and a week before they finally took off and disappeared from the area in which they had been released. Although they had only been away from the sea for a matter of hours in some cases, it seemed that they needed time to find their bearings again.

The oddest thing about that holiday was that as the car was drawing to a halt outside our cottage at the end of our return journey, we heard the phone ringing. John went in to answer it while the children and I tumbled out of the car. 'What's the matter?' I asked when I saw his face.

'I've got to go down and pick up another bird,' he said.

'That's all right, isn't it?'

'The man described it to me. He knows what he's talking about. I think it's another Manx shearwater.'

It was. It seemed ironical that, having released all

those shearwaters in Pembroke, we should return home and find another one virtually on our doorstep.

The people who had brought us this new shearwater called to see how it was getting on a few days later. It was then that they told us how they had found it. They had been going home from a party early one morning, and had seen this bird sitting at the side of the main road. They had stopped to examine it. There did not seem to be anything wrong with it so they took it down to the Grantham Canal and put it on the water. They had not been able to identify the bird and so on the next day they had called at the library and had looked it up. As soon as they realized that it was a shearwater, they had hurried back to the spot where they had left it. It was still there – except that it had drifted a few feet out from the bank and was now out of reach. Having tied some sticks together, they managed to draw it into the side, and later brought it to us. We put it on a course of antibiotics and by the end of the week it was quite fit. We could now make preparations to return it to the sea.

By this time a second shearwater had been brought in. This one had been picked up on the same night as the first. It had been found in Coventry High Street.

Shearwaters usually fly at night, using the stars for navigation. On cloudy nights they sometimes lose their way, and may be attracted by the bright lights of towns and motorways. The second shearwater had a badly cut wing. It would be at least ten days before we could let it go so we decided to keep them together.

They were no trouble – except that it took a long time to feed them. Nothing we did would persuade them to pick up food. They swam quite happily round in the bath three times a day, but they would not even look at the tempting sprats we threw in the water. Eventually we had to force-feed them. One of them took the food without any trouble at all but the other tried the same trick that those very first shearwaters we kept had played. It waited with the food in its beak and as soon as we looked away, it would shuffle backwards, and fall to the ground (if we did not catch it in time), shaking its head from side to side so that everyone and everything was spattered with minced fish – even the ceiling. If at first you do not succeed...

The two shearwaters stayed with us for six weeks. The cut on the second bird's wing had been much deeper than we had realized, but soon they were in beautiful condition and it was time for them to go.

Manx shearwaters have the most extraordinary homing instincts. You read reports of them having been taken to America and North Africa and still finding their way back to the breeding colonies. At first we were given advice on similar lines: that if we returned shearwaters to the sea, they would find their way back to their own colonies. In actual fact, ringed birds which have been recovered show that this does not happen. On one occasion, we have had to try to refind one bird which we released in the English Channel because it simply stayed where we had left it, swimming round and round and making no attempt to fly, dive or move in any particular direction. Could their experiences with us have dulled their natural instincts? I doubt it. Given time and the correct stimulation, they should be able to return without difficulty – provided that they have not been in captivity for too long.

By coincidence, the two birds were released from the

very beach where we had taken those eighteen shearwaters years before. They were taken out by boat to a spot some half a mile from land, and put into the water. We generally put a spot of dye on the birds so that we can recognize them again. Mr Swann (who does some release work for us) tossed some sprats towards them and, although they had not taken them at home, they took them readily enough in the sea. For the next five days they accepted food that was thrown towards them, remaining in the spot where they had been left for nine days. When the boat went out on the tenth day, there was no sign of our two – although there were plenty of shearwaters sweeping over the sea. We could only hope that ours were among them. Wild birds will, given time, accept one or two which have been newly released from captivity. If we release more than that number, they tend to keep themselves apart, swimming and living in a smaller, separate colony for a much longer time.

CHAPTER SEVEN: The Rabbit

It is strange how animals and birds can, at times, turn up in the most unexpected places. We have acquired several wild rabbits where we least expected to.

John and I were giving a lecture at a university to a large group of people. Having arrived a little late, we had to organize ourselves as quickly as possible. I saw one of the students draw John aside as we went in and whisper in his ear. John nodded and the student signalled to someone across the room. He then whispered something else. My curiosity was aroused but I did not have time to question John. We were giving a serious talk on the importance of birds in the development of the English language, explaining how such a word as 'boozing' has come to mean someone who drinks a lot but was once a term used exclusively to describe the drinking habits of birds; how hag and haggard come from words which once applied to an old hawk. Several times when we looked towards that student, he winked at us and that really put me off my stride.

When we were having a drink later with the director, John said,

'There are some students outside who want us to take three rabbits home with us.'

'Dead ones?' I asked, thinking of the food supply.

'No, they're only young ones, but no one's to know

they've got them.'

I could not imagine why anyone had to be so secretive about three rabbits. I found out later. We said goodbye to everyone and went out to the car where the students were waiting for us. We went round to the back of the hall of residence and up a flight of stairs to one of the student's rooms. At last I understood.

Two of the girls had moved their beds in together, and had filled the floor of the empty room with hay. In the middle of the hay three tiny baby rabbits were playing. I guessed that they were no more than six weeks old, and was a little surprised when the girls informed us that they had had them for six weeks. It seemed that they had been out for a walk and had found them scattered on the grass. From the way in which the students described them – pink and bald, tiny and blind – they must have only just been born. Having brought them back they had reared them on milk and cereals which they had taken from the dining room. Hot water bottles had kept them warm; an alarm clock buried in the hay had replaced the sound of their mother's heart beat. The rabbits had thrived; in fact, they seemed to be in wonderful condition. The students' only problem had been the staff. They had gone to all sorts of trouble to make sure that the housekeeper did not discover the rabbits, and now that they had reached the age when they could run about; things were clearly getting out of hand. The students seemed very relieved to pass the three animals over to us.

They were no trouble at all. They lapped the milk we gave them and ate every piece of green stuff with such speed that we wondered how such small animals could eat so much. The only difficulty was that, having been brought up in such unnaturally warm surroundings, we had to keep them indoors for a time because it was too wet and cold to put them into an outdoor run. So we kept them in the house and gradually reduced the heat. I soon discovered what the students had meant by problems.

All three of those animals had minds of their own. The first thing they had decided was that they were not going to stay in any box we provided. When we put a heavy weight on the top which we knew they would not be able to move, they used their teeth, nibbled a hole in the side of the box, and escaped in that way. Unfortunately, half the time we did not know that they were out, and they would appear when we least expected them.

John's boss came over for a meal one day. I had laid the table. Everything, I thought, looked just as it should. Our meal was to be salad with ham and eggs. You can imagine how I felt when we went into the dining-room and found two of those rabbits up on the table, nibbling the lettuce leaves. One of them was actually sitting in the plate of ham; and even the hard-boiled eggs had been chewed around the edges. It really put our visitor off: he would not eat a thing – not even the egg and bacon which we finally ended up eating.

One day the largest of the three disappeared altogether. We searched everywhere; in the end I decided it must have found its way outside. When Sophie sat down to play the piano that afternoon, however, the rabbit appeared quickly enough. It had been lying buried in the foliage of the plant which I kept on top of the piano. In fact, it must have been there all the time we had been looking. It had stayed so still, and had been so well camouflaged against the earth that we had all walked right by it without realizing that it was there.

Even living in unnatural surroundings indoors, it was fascinating to watch their wild instincts develop. These rabbits simply could not be compared with the pet ones we kept in the garden. They developed early in life an ability to lie still for a long time; they soon learned to sink down and remain absolutely motionless when there was an unusual noise; and they would completely disappear if a stranger turned up. They violently objected to being picked up. When we put them in the outside run, they became unmanageable. Like everything else, they needed time to adapt before they were freed. We also feared that they might be in danger from cats. We need not have bothered: they seemed to know that cats meant danger and kept well clear of them. We fixed a kind of funnel to the cage so that they could run in and out without the cats following them. Two of them never returned. We stumbled across one of them in the fields a few weeks later. When it saw us, it sunk down to the ground in the same way that it had done in our lounge. The smallest one stayed in the run for several days, but followed its brothers to freedom eventually.

These three left us much more easily than the last wild rabbit we had looked after.

This one, too, had also arrived when we least expected it. John and I had gone up to London for a dinner. As usual, we had had to rush to arrive there on time. It was my fault. I had flown one of the kestrels without weighing it first and checking that it would come back all right. Of course, it had flown straight to the top of the nearest elm tree, settled itself on one leg, and made it quite clear that it intended to stay there. I tried to coax it down with all sorts of tit-bits but it was simply not interested. We stood there looking at each other. I willed that bird to come back to my fist; he fluffed up his feathers and made it clear that he was staying exactly where he was. Normally, when I flew him, he came back to the fist almost as soon as I threw him off: in fact, he was so quick to return that the children called him Yo-yo.

Eventually, I could not wait for him any longer. I was worried about leaving him out all night, but I did not have any choice. I ran back to the house and as soon as that kestrel thought I was disappearing, he flew after me, calling out in panic. Minutes later, he was safely back on his perch.

As a result, we set off much later than we ought to have done. Everyone was already seated at the table when we reached the hotel. We crept in and were shown to our places. Almost as soon as John had sat down, he stood up again.

'What's the matter?' I hissed.

'There's something stuck in my trousers.'

'What sort of thing?'

'I don't know, but it's blooming uncomfortable.'

We did not have time to say anything else because the people on the top table came in. When we sat down again, John began to fiddle with something in the region of his trousers until he produced a brown object. He held it up triumphantly.

'What is it?'

'A clothes peg.'

In the rush, I must have left it in when I pressed his shirt.

It was at precisely this moment that the man opposite us leaned forward and said,

'The lady at the end of the table asks if you'd like a rabbit.'

'What sort of a rabbit?' I asked.

'Dead or alive?' said John.

Messages passed up and down the table for a bit until we came to an arrangement to see the lady afterwards. It proved to be a wild rabbit. The lady had found it when she had gone to stay in the country one weekend. It had been tiny: so small, in fact, that she did not think she would be able to rear it. She had succeeded, however, and it had now been with her for nearly a year. The only problem was that she did not know what to do with it next. She wanted to return it to the country so that it could lead a natural life; she knew, however, that you simply could not leave it out in the middle of a field and expect it to survive. She had tried to release it herself, but when she had returned to see how it was getting on, the rabbit had run up to her, and its eyes had expressed such pathetic misery that she had taken it home again.

We returned home with her after the dinner. She had explained that the rabbit had complete freedom of movement in her flat, so I suppose, therefore, that we should have known what to expect. What she had not told us, however, was that the ten other rabbits, the six guinea pigs, the two tortoises and the cat, all had equal freedom. It was a tiny fifth-floor flat and its only pretence to a garden was a window-box. Everywhere we looked there were animals – or evidence of them. The lady had further complicated matters by marrying a husband who disliked animals.

Of all the animals in that flat, the wild one made its presence felt much more than any of the others. All the others seemed settled and placid; the brown rabbit, on the other hand, was half as big as the others but twenty times as energetic.

It ran round and round that flat, dashing from room to room and jumping right over anything that got in its way. It would stop as suddenly as it had started and lie on the floor. Occasionally, it sprung right up into the air without any warning at all, and when it was airborne it would kick with its hind legs so that it looked as though it were practising some complicated kind of ballet step.

It is most disconcerting to have a conversation in the full knowledge that, every so often, a rabbit will tear through the room like an express train. It seemed to regard John as a spring board: it would run up his back and spring off his shoulder. You ought to have seen John's face the first time it did that. The lady gave us cups of coffee but it was not easy to sit and drink them: the rabbit would run up our legs, and almost knock the cups out of our hands. Once or twice it dashed into the room and tried to screech to a halt in front of us. Unfortunately, the rug on which it was travelling would be carried across the floor by the speed of its movement, and we would watch the animal disappear as fast as it had appeared.

What had hastened the decision that this rabbit must go was the fact that it had started to sharpen its teeth on the furniture. I thought the table looked a bit worse-for-wear when we came in. The rabbit had sharpened its teeth so effectively on two of the legs that they had broken off. Her husband had had to cut down the other legs to match them. Two of the chairs had received the same treatment; the sideboard looked badly in need of similar treatment: it had developed a very lop-sided appearance.

It was not, of course, the rabbit's fault. All rodents have teeth that grow all the time, and they have to gnaw something hard to keep them short. In the wild it would have chewed twigs and hard stalks; in captivity, it had to find a substitute.

Understandably, the husband's dislike of animals had become an obsession. The rabbit *had* to go. We calmly agreed to take it home with us if they had a box we could put it in. They found the box quickly enough; catching the rabbit was a different matter altogether. As far as he was concerned, we had created a new game; in the end all four of us were crawling around the floor in pursuit. At one point, we all swore that we had seen him go under a chair. We surrounded it and gingerly reached beneath it to pull him out. He was not there. He was sitting on the seat, looking down at our activity with the greatest interest. When we caught sight of him, he jumped right over our heads and ran into the kitchen. Time and time again he would wait until one of us had slowly reached out and was just about to grab him. He would then skip out of the way and run off again. We were beginning to get really cross with him: he had the laugh on us every time.

Eventually, John had a brainwave.

'Sit down,' he said, 'carry on talking, and pretend he isn't there. His curiosity will get the better of him.'

So we sat down again and, sure enough, the rabbit peered round the corner of John's chair, not seeming to understand why we had finished the chasing game. John simply reached down, picked him up and put him in the box before the animal knew what was happening.

He did not like captivity. He scratched and scrabbled, but he could not get out. We had tied it up too well for that. He objected all the way back in the car.

We put him in the Morant hutch when we got home. These are long and triangular, completely enclosed with wire, and have a sleeping box at the end. The rabbit can eat the grass which grows through the wire, and the hutch can easily be moved on to fresh grass when necessary.

For the first few days that rabbit was really puzzled by the big outside world. If there was any unusual noise, it would dash back into its box and burrow into the hay. A few seconds later, that twitching nose would be poking round the corner, and a very enquiring rabbit would follow it. It would then sit in the middle of its run, as if asking whether things were really as bad as they sounded. At first, its reaction to anything it saw for the first time – whether it be the children on their bikes, cars going up the road or our two dogs – was the same: it nearly drove him mad. It did not take him long to realize, however, that nothing could touch him in the safety of his hutch.

As soon as he had discovered that fact, he began to really torment the two dogs. We have had all sorts of animals and birds in the centre including rabbits wild and tame, but none of them has ever had the effect on the dogs that this one had. They seemed to be drawn towards it like a magnet. We had two dogs: a big, soft English setter, and a light-footed little whippet whom we had always called Puppy, although she was now ten years old. When the rabbit saw the dogs he ran up and down, up and down, inviting them to come and play. The dogs ran up and down and round and round as well, making bigger and bigger circles until they were dashing around the garden as if they had been scalded. Sometimes they went right round the cottage, and we wondered whatever was happening. They were always drawn back to the rabbit hutch. They stayed near it for hours, bouncing up and down, barking, trying to get round the hutch as quickly as they could, chasing the rabbit they could not reach. At least, Puppy did; the setter was a bit too large to take the corners with any speed, and he generally finished head over heels in the flower bed.

We had promised faithfully that the rabbit would have his freedom, and after three weeks in captivity, we made a hole large enough for it to get through. It had taken us this long to wean him from the food he had been eating in London. The lady who had owned him had always given him dry food because he made less mess when she gave him that. He was not, however, going to find bowls of dry, rolled oats in the country, and our first job had been to teach him to recognize natural food. That seemed easy enough: he was prepared to try anything. The problem was that, not having had fresh food before, it made him ill. He scoured for two days, and we became genuinely worried about him. We restricted him to blackberry leaves, which seemed to help a great deal. It was a relief when, on the third day, we watched him dash up and down his run as cheekily as ever. We gave him a little less dry food each day until he did not need it any more.

It was then that we opened up the hole in his run and stood back to watch how he would cope with the big outside world. His nose came out of the hole pretty quickly. We stood and watched it twitching. He sat like that for ten minutes. Then he hopped out through the hole, lolloped over to the front door which we had left open, into the lounge and on to the settee. He settled down there and looked very pleased with himself.

That was the last thing we had expected him to do. So had the dogs. They sat and barked with real indignation. The rabbit sat on the cushion and looked down at them. He seemed to know that he was perfectly safe while we were there. He was right: we would not have dared to leave him alone with those dogs. I would never have trusted them. When we went out we put the rabbit back in his hutch.

John began to grumble because he now had to set about making another door. He had made a hole in the first one, thinking that the rabbit would be free to go in and out at will; but if its whole idea in coming out was to make itself comfortable in our lounge, that was a different matter altogether.

We soon learned that he was quite capable of looking after himself as far as the dogs were concerned. He would inspect the garden when we were out there, but if there was an unusual noise or anything else that startled him, he would be through that front door and in an easy chair as quick as lightning. One day, he discovered he could go right round the cottage and arrive back where he started. That was fun. He went round and round the cottage, running faster and faster until I became dizzy just watching him.

Every time he went out now, whatever the weather, he made several circuits of the cottage before he came indoors. That journey really excited him. Sometimes he would spring high up in the air, giving that extra airborne kick which we had seen at the lady's flat.

'The rabbit's ballet step,' Sophie called it, and that is just what it looked like.

It was soon after this that he began to torment the dogs. The two dogs had become used to him as part of the scenery and did not bother with him. That did not suit the rabbit: if running up and down did not excite them, it would not take him long to think of some game that did. He started by running towards them and leaping right over their backs; if they slept on, he jumped on to the setter and used his back as a spring board. He never took the same liberties with Puppy: he seemed to appreciate that he had to be much more careful with her. Good-natured old Sam, however, although there was a lot of him, would not have hurt a fly.

It was more than the dogs could stand: they would start to give chase. He enjoyed that and would lead them right round the cottage and back to the front door. Then round again they would go, and again and again. He would lead them round that circuit six or seven times, and when he was sure that the two dogs had got into the habit of it, he would sit on the front doorstep and watch them go round and round and round. They would often do another half dozen circuits before they realized that they were chasing thin air.

The rabbit knew that he was not allowed to stay in the house at night and that when we were getting ready for bed, the first thing we did was to put him back in his hutch. We meant to anyway: but he would disappear in anticipation. All evening he would have been sitting on his favourite cushion; when we went to pick him up, he was no longer there. Knowing he would be in the house somewhere, we searched high and low in all sorts of places: in drawers which had been shut and behind the curtains for example. That rabbit had completely disappeared. In the morning, he would be sitting on the door mat, looking very pleased with himself.

That became the pattern: however often we watched him and however hard we looked, we could never discover where he was hiding.

We found out one day unexpectedly. John was playing the piano. I was outside and saw the old Colonel coming down the hill with his Great Dane. They both look pretty fierce, but neither of them are once you get to know them. The rabbit, of course, did not know that. He took one look at the pair of them and ran. John said he wondered what was happening. One minute he was peacefully playing the piano and the next a rabbit tore through his legs, squeezed through the narrow gap between the wall and the piano and climbed through the hole in the back. We had found his favourite hiding place: our piano. He had made himself very comfortable in there, too, with Sophie's jumper to lie on.

It was not long before he started to vanish outside, too. He would stay away for a day or two at a time but we did not worry because we knew he would always come back again. We had been a bit worried about the traffic on the road at first but he seemed to know that it meant danger and he would sit in the long grass on the verge before attempting to cross. He earned top marks for his road drill.

We were having a cup of tea on the lawn one day when John said, 'There's something moving across the field. If you look carefully you can see the corn moving in a line.'

The corn was about three-quarters grown then and had reached the stage where it seemed to be moving all the time; where the slightest wind would cause the long stalks to sway, and start a wave of motion that ran across the whole field. At the top of the rise we could see the corn folding back in a sharp line which divided this gentle swaying motion. Something was making a path through it. As we watched, the line came nearer and nearer until it reached the hedge immediately opposite us, finishing at a narrow gap. Out of the gap popped the rabbit – as cheerful as ever.

That hole in the hedge became his favourite gap. We would often see him going through it or returning the same way. We used to look out for the lines he wove through the growing corn; for as the crop reached maturity the rabbit's path became more and more obvious.

We never knew when he was going to appear. He would often pop out from the piano when someone started to play. Once Sophie pulled back her bed covers before getting into bed and out popped the rabbit: he had found himself another comfortable spot. Aunt Gertrude nearly sat on him once. She had not seen him sitting on the cushion – well, she had not thought of looking. Once I bent down to take the plates out of the cupboard and felt something soft. It gave me a start. It was the rabbit, of course, but when you were not expecting to come into contact with something alive, it comes as something of a shock.

The gardener on the estate had the biggest surprise of all. He did not like rabbits. They were a nuisance in the garden and made more work for him. He came across to us one day, looking very pale.

'You'll never guess but I've seen a mighty peculiar

thing,' he said. 'My dog is a real good rabbiter, and she got wind of this one up the hedge. When she chased it, the rabbit didn't run away at all. It ran down into the house and jumped into the wife's lap. She was sitting by the fire knitting. It gave her quite a turn; made her drop all her stitches. It's done the same thing once or twice since. I've never known a thing like it.'

We had though; we knew where that rabbit had come from.

He was growing more and more independent every day. At first he had loved to be with the children but now he did not bother about them any more. His visits to us became rarer and rarer. It seemed that he only came home when he wanted to torment the dogs. He had grown a lot during that summer and was a much more muscular animal than the one we had brought back from London with us.

Autumn came – and so did myxomatosis. The lady who had given him to us had told us that she had had him immunized against the disease. We hoped it would be effective. I could not have endured the thought of that cheeky rabbit suffering as the wild ones were. I thought he had more chance than the others because he had never shown any inclination to burrow. He seemed much happier lying *on* something than inside it. It is when rabbits are in their burrows that they transfer the disease to each other: for the fleas which live on the fur carry it. The wild rabbits themselves seem to appreciate this fact: I have found several litters of rabbits which have been born above ground in nesting places which resemble forms. We did not see our rabbit after that wave of the disease. We felt sad, sure in our own hearts that he must have died.

We had our first heavy frost on Christmas Eve that

year: everything was glittering white and silver. When I went out on to our front doorstep, the first thing I saw was the rabbit, looking very sorry for himself. I thought he wanted to go indoors at first, but when I opened the door he did not enter. When I threw out the corn for the hens, however, he bounded over and ate it hungrily. He ate the stale bread too. He had known where to come when he was hungry. After that, he took to visiting us from time to time throughout the winter, generally when it had been cold.

It was the end of March when we saw him for the last time. He had come across to the cottage and had eaten some bread and corn. As I stood there watching him, he crossed the road and went through his favourite gap in the hedge. Across the ploughed land he went, jumping into the air and giving that funny, characteristic kick of his. I watched him until I could not see him any more. It was not that he was out of range. His fur was shaded in such a way that it acted as a perfect camouflage against the ploughed earth and he did not show up. I did not know as I stood there watching him that I would not see him again. But I will always remember thinking how perfectly he had learned to fit into his own world.

CHAPTER EIGHT: The Guillemot

Gilly is special. Gilly is a guillemot, but he does not think he is a bird at all. He thinks he is a little man. In fact, he thinks more than that. He thinks he is one of the family, and the most important member of it. If he is left out of anything, he makes such a fuss that we have to go and get him straight away. Gilly has been with us for six years now, but it only took him a few days to worm his way into our affections. He means a lot to us, does Gilly.

We have cared for a lot of guillemots in our time: over five hundred in all. Every one of them has come to us because of the effect of oil. I was horrified – and intrigued – the first time. This bird had landed in the back garden of someone who lived thirty miles from the coast. What was more, the bird was so coated with oil that it was difficult to distinguish one feather from another. We had not received an oiled bird before and we phoned all sorts of people for advice. Everyone told us the same thing: it would be kindest to destroy the bird. If it had been oiled, it did not stand a chance of survival.

That kind of statement is like a red rag to a bull as far as we are concerned. It is so easy to destroy. To destroy life is one of the most final and efficient things a man can do. Yet with all his superior knowledge, man cannot create life; the least he can do is to endeavour to save it, and he has a responsibility to himself and all living things – to do so. The world may be getting top heavy with human beings, but we should remember that animals and birds and plants have as much right to survive as ourselves. The world would be a poorer place without them. When anyone looks at an animal and tells me that the kindest thing would be to destroy it, well it makes me angry: nine times out of ten they mean not that it would be the kindest thing at all, but rather the easiest and the cheapest – which is a different matter altogether. I am not claiming we never destroy anything that is brought to us: if it is suffering, or if it is so badly injured that there is no hope of its ever resuming a normal life, then we do put it to sleep. But this is a decision we never make ourselves. It is the vet who decides, for he is the one with the knowledge and the experience to judge; if he thinks the creature has a chance of survival, we try to give it that chance.

Nobody would give us any encouragement whatsoever with an oiled bird. In fact, the opposite was the case: we were abused for trying. The attitude taken was that there were so many guillemots around the British coast that the loss of a few of them would do no harm whatsoever.

We kept that first guillemot alive for two weeks. It died on Christmas morning. I was genuinely upset about it. Within two weeks I had grown very fond of the bird. It had fought for its life, and we had thought it was going to make it. Then, on Christmas morning, we had found it dead in its box. In the next few years, we often cared for oiled birds, and although we would not have admitted defeat, we could have counted the number on one hand which had survived long enough to be reintroduced to the sea.

Half the trouble was that the people who picked them up had washed them. It is a natural enough reaction. They had found a filthy bird and, wanting to help it, they had cleaned it. It was obvious early on that these cleaned birds had far less chance of survival than those which came to us in their dirty state. We put the call out that if oiled birds were to be brought to us it was vitally important that they should not be washed. Washing robs a bird's feathers of its natural oils, and upsets the lay of the feathers. The bird loses its natural waterproofing, is no longer protected from the weather, and has no means of getting itself warm. When returned to the water, they became completely waterlogged. Even after two moults (approximately two years) there were not many that could swim for more than half an hour without the water soaking into their feathers. By that time they had become so used to captivity that it seemed cruel to return them to the sea at all.

For ten years we worked on these oiled birds, taking countless notes and getting nowhere near the success we were sure we ought to achieve. There was a small group of us by this time, all amateurs, and we were collectively seeking the answers. We studied not only the guillemots which were brought to us but their patterns of behaviour in the wild: how they fished, and how long they needed to stay beneath the water at any one time. We had some wonderful days watching them in their natural environment, and when we returned home to our sick ones, it made us more determined than ever to solve the problem. We spent some time at Dunstanbrough Head in Northumberland. This was a wonderful spot: the water was so clear that we could lie on top of the cliffs and watch the guillemots diving and fishing, seeing every movement without any trouble at all. They move beautifully beneath the water, twisting, turning, floating in a kind of aquatic ballet. All four of us were absolutely captivated by them. As they submerged, their feathers seemed to hold a pocket of air round them, just like otters do. We knew then that the lie of the feathers was as important to the bird as its waterproofing.

It was not until young Andrew Greenwood went to veterinary college at Cambridge that we made a real breakthrough. He arranged for post mortems to be made on every bird that died at no cost to ourselves. We had had post mortems done before but they were expensive. The results which we obtained from the numbers we could afford to have carried out professionally were too slight to be conclusive. Now we really began to obtain answers. The birds which we were losing were dying of kidney failure, and there was oil in their gut. One bird which had been with us for a year was found to have had its gut completely blocked by oil. It was obvious that the problem was not so much one of removing the oil from their feathers, but flushing it out of their insides. We gradually worked out a programme which began to achieve positive results. One member of our group collected the birds in Portsmouth. As soon as they were picked up, they were put into cloth bags with a handful of fuller's earth. This kept the birds warm, and prevented them from struggling and suffering shock. By the time I had picked them up, the fuller's earth had removed much of the surplus oil. As soon as we had them home we cleaned the eyes and nostrils. They were kept in constant heat and allowed to wash and preen as much as they wanted. Each day they were dosed with liquid paraffin until there was no longer any sign of oil in their droppings. One problem bedevilled us for a long time: the state of the birds' legs and feet. They peeled and became very sore. We thought it was the effect of the oil which had burned them. We purchased all kinds of medicinal creams and ointments and, although they helped, they were not the answer.

The trouble seemed to start where the feather line stopped at the top of the leg. The knee joint would become so swollen at times that it seemed almost arthritic. We found the answer by chance. Someone sent us a paper written by a man at Basle Zoo on the importance of diet to captive birds. It set us thinking, and eventually we found the answer: a small element called thiamine. Thiamine is stored in the liver and it is only found in fresh food. As soon as a fish is caught, its thiamine content begins to disappear until within twenty-four hours it is virtually non-existent. Predators need this element for their own health and a thiamine deficient diet will eventually make them ill. It generally shows up in the skin and the feet. For such fish-eating birds as guillemots the subject is further complicated by the fact that some fish, being deficient in thiamine themselves, absorb the element that is in the bird's body. The result is that even if you dose a bird up with thiamine and then feed it the wrong species of fish, it can still show the same signs of thiamine deficiency.

Still, we had found the last piece of our puzzle and we had at last reached the stage where we could reintroduce oiled birds to the sea five weeks after we had received them. Unfortunately it was still too long: behaviour is not static. It changes to fit the environment in which an animal finds itself; it changes to suit changing conditions. In five weeks a bird will have started to adapt its behaviour to the conditions imposed by captivity. We were, however, finding the answers and although it took several weeks to get them back into the sea, they were going back and were surviving.

Their chance of survival had no correlation with the degree of oiling in the first place. It was only by chance again that we discovered this fact. There had been a bad oiling incident in the Channel and I had gone down to help with the birds. Before I left, John had sat down and worked out how many we could afford to look after. A guillemot can eat a pound of fish a day and if you have ten birds which cost thirty pence a day, there is little money left in the bank. We also had to consider such additional costs as electricity, travel, etc. John said we could take six. When I got down to the coast and saw those pathetic oiled-up birds, I wanted to take them all. I put twelve in the car, each one wrapped up in its bag like a neat parcel. Then I saw the others which the men were discarding. They were so badly oiled that they were hardly recognizable as birds at all. They would all be destroyed. As I drove home, I could not erase the picture of those pathetic creatures from my mind. I turned the car round, went back and chose twelve of the very bad ones.

John was not very pleased when I turned up with four times as many birds as we could afford to look after. I explained, however, that I doubted whether any of the bad cases would survive the night. Miraculously, they did. We saved nine of the dozen lightly oiled birds. We saved all twelve of the others. The twenty-one birds were all released from the same beach in Cornwall six weeks later.

Gilly was never oiled. One day Martin Smailes phoned us up from Flamborough Head. Would we take a guillemot? Of course we would. What was wrong with it? Nothing at all.

'Do you just want me to get it straight down to the release pens?' I asked.

'If you like,' he answered.

When John came home and I told him, he said, 'That's odd. If there's nothing wrong with it, why don't they take it out in the lifeboat like they do everything else and let it go? I'd better phone up and see what it's all about.'

He was grinning when he came back. It seemed they had taken it out many times, but Gilly had a mind of his own. He was not going to live in the sea any longer. If he was not back on the beach by the time they got back, he would have landed soon after.

John fetched Gilly the next day. He was late getting back. 'Is the bird all right?' I asked.

'I should think so. He's not stopped talking all the way home.'

I could hear him. Despite the fact that he was still in a box, he was determined to let us all know that he had arrived. His harsh, strident call went on and on. 'Have you had that all the way home?' I asked.

'It hasn't stopped,' John said.

He brought the box into the kitchen, opened it and out jumped Gilly. He stood in the middle of the rug and, loudly protesting his indignation, flapped his stubby little wings at the same time. He looked very grand. Every guillemot we had received before had been oiled up and dirty; this one was beautiful, standing up like a long-beaked miniature penguin. His wings, back and head were black; his front was pure white. He stood there for a second looking like a waiter waiting for his orders. Only there was no question of waiting with Gilly: he had arrived and was here to stay.

The children were playing in the lounge with their friends from the farm next door. They were laughing about something. Gilly stood up a little straighter, and inclined his head to one side and then the other so that his long neck looked like a question mark. As soon as he had worked out where that noise was coming from, he was off to investigate. He waddled into the lounge, flapping his wings and calling out in excitement. We always have one bird or another indoors. I suppose that the children are so used to them that having another one walking round the place makes little difference.

'Where's he come from?' Sophie asked casually as she shook a dice.

John started to explain, but Gilly took the matter into his own hands. He was not going to be left out of anything. Before anyone realized what he was doing, he had jumped on to the stool and then on to the table, tipping board, cards and counters all over the floor. He then called out as if to say: 'There you are! That serves you right for not taking any notice of me!'

The children were astonished by Gilly's behaviour – but not cross in the way in which Martin Smailes (the friend who had given him to us) had been when some holidaymakers had found him when he was still a tiny, fluffy chick.

'It's the same every year,' he said. 'If only people would leave young birds alone they'd be all right. The adults would find them.'

I have my doubts with guillemots. They seem to breed in such daft places; narrow ledges on high cliffs, for example. I have often wondered how the birds manage to stay there. It must be much worse for eggs or newly hatched chicks. Mind you, guillemot eggs are more triangular in shape than other birds' eggs, and that stops them rolling. They get covered in sticky bird droppings which, I suppose, acts like glue and keeps them on the ledges. All the same, a lot of eggs do fall off and smash on the rocks and I am pretty sure that Gilly is not the first young guillemot to have fallen from a nesting ledge. The ledges these birds choose are narrow enough at the best of times but, as if that is not enough, they seem to wedge themselves against each other like travellers in a tube train during the rush hour. They are not outstanding parents at the best of times, they are too interested in a communal life to protect their own youngster. I have seen a guillemot brood three different chicks, one after the other. Whether it could not recognize its own chick or was just feeling maternal I shall never know.

What had happened to Gilly I do not know. Perhaps he had been pushed off the crowded ledge – on the other hand, he may have fallen off or decided to try and fly before he had any feathers. Malcolm had not thought to ask the family exactly where they had found him, and nobody knew how long ago it had been picked up. But there was nothing left for it: the Smailes had a young guillemot to rear and they made a good job of it. Guillemots are sociable birds at the best of times and Gilly was no exception. The only difference was that instead of spending all his time with other guillemots he liked to stay with people and he liked children best of all – particularly girls.

As soon as he was fully fledged the Smailes had taken him back to the sea. But he was much more concerned about keeping an eye on the family than returning to the water. He did not appreciate the sea at all: the waves running over the shingle frightened him and he shouted at it. When it still kept coming, he flapped his wings and got as far away from it as he could. The only way to coax Gilly into the water was for the Smailes to swim themselves. (They told us that they had never swum as much in their lives before as they did that year.) Even then Gilly liked to be sure that they were always in sight.

As the summer advanced, they took him right out to sea and left him where the wild guillemots congregated. When they returned to shore and started to pull the boat up the beach, a very indignant Gilly would come running over. He had arrived before them and had been impatiently waiting for their return. That happened several times. They even had friends take him out and leave him in the sea. Gilly could not understand that at all. He would find his way back to the beach where all the holidaymakers were sunbathing and would go up to each of them in turn, calling out and flapping his wings. He was looking for the Smailes. In the end somebody picked him up and took him back to them.

When the autumn came, things began to get difficult. Fish were hard to come by and nobody felt like swimming so that Gilly could take his exercise ...

Which brings us back to Gilly's entry into our family. Exercise was still a problem: he had to make do with the bath, which he did not like one bit. He would stretch out his neck and call and call. He would only quieten down when we spoke to him. John had the answer.

'You know, I think he wants one of us to get in with him.'

We persuaded Sophie to take off her socks and shoes and paddle in the water.

As soon as she did this, Gilly was happy. He bathed and splashed with such vigour that even the ceiling got wet. He dipped his head under the water and stretched right up again in a snake-like movement. Sophie got so wet that she might just as well have stripped off and had her own bath at the same time. We fared little better – in spite of the fact that we had had time to cover ourselves with towels. Getting into the bath with Gilly became Sophie's regular job for a day or two; but by the end of the week, the bird knew that the bath was fun, and did not mind going in on his own. Nevertheless he always preferred company.

Sometimes I put him in the bath while I made the beds or cleaned the bedrooms. Gilly would swim round and eat a few fish, but if I took time to sit on the side of the bath and talk to him, he would really show off: splashing, jumping, and getting so excited sometimes that he jumped right out of the bath, and landed in the middle of the rug. He would then look round in a surprised sort of way, wondering how the water had disappeared so suddenly.

The trouble is that our toilet is right next to the bath. Sometimes I leave Gilly in the bath and forget to tell people he is there. Of course, as soon as Gilly thinks he has company, he starts showing off again, splashing everyone and everything. As a result one or two visitors have had rather unfortunate experiences. One old lady was so wet that she had to change completely and borrow clothes from me to go home.

Young eagle owl

A simple conjuring trick, if you know how!

Only a grass snake!

Manx shearwater

Feeding time for hedgehogs

Keeping a tight hold on that fox!

Gilly joins in the game!

'Come and play with me?' Sophie and the young eagle owl

Gilly is curious about everything. He has to come and look at anyone who calls at the house, and if anyone is standing at the back door, Gilly will go and peck the visitor's feet if he does not like the look of him. If sick birds are brought in, we always put them in a cardboard box until we are sure that they are not suffering from shock. Gilly investigates every box he can find – and the contents. I always worry that his long beak peeping over the edge might finish a lot of our patients off.

When we go on holiday, friends of ours who keep a shop look after Gilly, and they say he is just as nosy with them. They fixed him up in an upstairs bedroom and left the door open a little so that he could hear their voices. The next thing Alma knew was that the customers were edging away from her and collecting in a knot just inside the door. She wondered what was happening until she saw Gilly walking across the floor and pecking a few feet before he went back and sat down beside her. After that, Gilly investigated every customer that called.

The next time that we took a holiday, Gilly walked right into that house and followed exactly the same routine as the year before, even going to the same dish for his food. We were amazed at his memory. But guillemots are intelligent: John used to arrange simple tests for the oiled ones which we looked after, and concluded that they had the ability to reason simply.

It is only intelligent creatures which play. Gilly plays: he plays with anything from a button to a piece of string. One day I kept losing him. When I went upstairs I knew where he had been: there was a mess all over my pillow and Gilly was sitting at the top of the bed tossing the light switch (it is on a long string) backwards and forwards, and trying to catch it again as it swung. He loves shiny things – bits of silver paper, for example – and he will toss what he has found up in the air and run after it. When he has caught it, he tosses it up again. He loves shoe laces and shiny buckles and will try to pull them off. People who call and see Gilly heading for their feet usually run away. They think he is attacking them – but he only wants their shoes. He likes cameras, too – especially if they have long, swinging straps. He loves to jump up and try to catch hold of them. He is intrigued by small cars which run along the ground and clockwork toys which turn round and round: but he soon gets bored with them. Balls, on the other hand, never bore him. We buy table tennis balls for him and he loves them, poking them with his beak and chasing after them when they shoot off across the room; trying to pick one up and, when he cannot do that, sitting on it – well, trying to sit on it. Perhaps he thinks that it is an egg. The problem is that it will never stay still when he wants it to: as he settles down on it, it shoots across the room and he has to run after it and start the whole exercise over again.

He likes balloons, too. We discovered that fact the first Christmas he was with us. Gilly nearly went mad when we started putting up the decorations. If the paper chains dropped, Gilly would be on to them immediately, pulling at them and tearing them if we did not snatch them away quickly enough. The Christmas tree which Sophie decorated was the biggest toy Gilly had ever seen. First of all he jumped up and pulled the baubles down. We then removed the lights because we were afraid that he might get an electric shock. He next turned his attention to the fairy on the top of the tree; all that week he was trying to get it down. One day there was a terrific crash and when we rushed into the dining room to see what had happened, the Christmas tree was lying on its side, the decorations and the earth from the bucket were scattered all over the floor and right in the middle of the mess stood Gilly. He had the decency to look subdued for a short time, but he soon forgot that the mess had anything to do with him. Picking up one of the decorations, he started to toss it into the air. He would have liked to play with the balloons as well and kept trying to jump up to them. In the end, St John unfastened one and let it float to the ground. Gilly was at it straight away and we all waited for the bang. We thought that his sharp beak would puncture it immediately – but it did not. He caught hold of the knotted end, shook it, threw it up into the air, and chased after it. He would play with a balloon for an hour at a time. He hardly ever punctured one: it was the children tossing them about the room which did that. Gilly like blue balloons best. If he was given a choice of colours, he would always choose the blue one. He preferred it when there were two or three of them tied together in a bunch.

He liked the counters and dice that the children used when they played ludo and other games of that kind, and he soon learned that they became angry when he stole them from the board. We would watch him. He would sit there watching the children, pretending to have no interest in the counters; then, when they least expected it, he would dive in, catch hold of a dice or something similar, and dash across the room. They would try to shut him outside when they wanted to play, but he would sit on the mat with his beak pressed against the door looking so sorry for himself that someone would usually relent and let him in. Sometimes he was very bad tempered when he was shut out: he would stand on the mat calling out so loudly that someone would have to let him in so that they could have a bit of peace.

The trouble was that Mrs Bellamy and Gilly did not see eye to eye. She thought he ought to be house-trained like the dogs, but it is rather difficult explaining that kind of thing to a bird. He seems to know. Sometimes when she is going upstairs, Gilly will go in front of her and make a mess on every stair. When she starts shouting and telling the bird what she thinks of him, Gilly disappears under a bed and waits until she has calmed down before he comes out. He often goes under the bed when he wants to get out of the way. If he is under there, it is usually an indication that he has done or taken something he ought not to have.

One day Grandma had come to stay. We were so busy talking that we forgot all about Gilly. We were woken up by piercing screams in the night and we dashed out to see what had happened: someone had been murdered at the very least. We had forgotten to put Gilly back in his box the night before and he had found a good spot under the spare bed. Grandma had decided to get up early and when she put her foot over the edge of the bed, Gilly had reached out and pecked her toes. It had given her a shock. The next time we had somebody staying, Gilly went one better than that. He jumped on the bed, lay down on the pillow and went to sleep right beside her. It was most unpleasant when he lifted his tail and made a mess right in the guest's eye.

We once took Gilly back to the sea, thinking that the

sea water would do him good. He started to aquaplane out to sea immediately, and soon disappeared from sight. We were very upset. He was so tame that we did not think he would know how to look after himself. We waited there for ages in case he came back, but there was no sign of him. Dad tried to convince us that now that he had felt the call of the sea, his other instincts would be roused and he would be able to fend for himself. All the same, we felt sad as we started to walk back towards the cliff. Suddenly, Sophie saw a commotion further down the beach and went off to see what was happening while we walked on. Then she shouted over to us and we ran to see what was the matter. It was Gilly.

He had landed on the wrong part of the beach and was running round calling and pecking feet as he searched for us. People had tried to push him back into the sea. Two youths were throwing stones at him. I suppose they thought that they would frighten him off. Sophie shouted to the guillemot just then. The bird called back with a loud cry and ran across the beach towards her. He must have been completely lost.

We were very careful with him after that, only letting him swim in the shallow pools and guarding the way to the sea. All the same, it was difficult to keep him on the land. Once he had the feel of a large expanse of water beneath him, he would half run, half flap, building up a terrific speed which carried him right across the sand. He moved much faster than we could run. I think he had learned his own lesson, though. When he did go into the sea, he did not go very far out and did not stay in for very long. He would regularly come out of the water and look to see where we were before having another swim. He did not intend to get lost again.

There is nothing at all wrong with Gilly. He is perfectly fit, and he is in a wonderful condition. He looks exactly like any wild guillemot, but he is not a wild bird at all. He may look like one but he does not behave like one. If we tried to release a bird as tame as he is, it would not survive. Not only has he never had the chance to develop the skills and instincts which he needs to survive, but he has never developed the patterns of behaviour of wild birds, and the wild guillemots would simply not accept him.

It is the same with people. We do not really like people who behave in an anti-social way or do things that we do not think are right. If we know people who are like that, we tend to avoid them. Animals are the same. They do not simply accept another one into their way of life because it looks like them; it has to behave like them as well. Not only will they not accept it, but they will object to it and harry it until it is driven right away. Sometimes they will attack and kill it. You cannot take a tame creature, put it out into the wild and expect it to survive. It is cruel to try.

There is no doubt that Gilly is tame; in fact, he does not think he is a bird at all. As I sit here listening to him flying up and down the stairs pretending to chase a fly, I have to agree with him.

CHAPTER NINE: The Badger

We have to be very careful with some of our animals. It is not only the truly wild ones that are a problem. Those that seem tame can be pretty treacherous, in fact they can be worst of all. With an adult wild deer or a fox, you know how they are likely to behave. You can understand what their reactions are going to be when you try and handle them, but you can never be sure with one that is supposed to be tame. Half the time they are not tame at all: they have simply learned to adapt their lives to include people. They have learned to lose their fear and mistrust of a human situation and they will often go and seek it out. They may appear tame but when some stimulus awakes a latent instinct, they will react as swiftly and as viciously as a wild creature.

I think crows are worst in this respect. Anyone who believes that he has tamed a crow should think twice before letting it loose in the country: they can be very dangerous. Not only have they lost their fear of people, but they are attracted towards them. If they do not obtain the reaction which they expect, they will stab out. A magpie can hurt, but a raven or a hooded crow really does puncture the skin. What is more, they are invariably attracted to bright objects and nine times out of ten they will go for the eyes. We knew of a six-week-old baby that had been attacked in its pram by a boy's tame crow. It had been attracted by the baby's toys. Unfortunately, the baby's mother did not know that and both of them needed hospital treatment.

I nearly lost my eye to a tame crow on one occasion. A young couple had reared it and had tried to release it on several occasions. The bird had found its way back home from as far as fifty miles away and it had reached the stage where, when they went out, the bird refused to get out of the car. It seemed to know that they were going to leave it there and it turned nasty when they tried to force it to leave the car. They lived in a bed-sitting room and it seemed that this crow was taking over more and more of their home and more and more of their lives.

They asked us whether we would take him. Jack the crow is a real character. We still have him – but we are very careful with him. He was tame from the word go. He had also developed a great liking for beer. One day he found a glass of beer. took a good drink, then turned round and flew at me, catching hold of my hair and stabbing at my face. I could not get him off. I thought that he had damaged one of my eyes; fortunately, he had stabbed just above and beneath it. All the same I carried the marks of that attack for a long time and I thought at the time that I would be scarred for life.

Since Jack was a tame bird, I was simply not prepared for the sudden change of character – but I could not blame Jack. However tame he may appear, he is basically a wild bird and no amount of human company can destroy his basic, wild instincts.

In an adult wild animal we are prepared for that kind of behaviour; we try to encourage and preserve it, doing all we can to prevent the animal becoming tame or learning to accept people in any way. We know that when it becomes fit enough to return to its own environment, it will be a truly wild creature which is returning, one which has retained its wild instincts and behavioural patterns, and not one which has become so used to a human environment that it is going to take a long time to reorientate itself.

As soon as an animal comes to us we have to decide what its chances are of being released again. If it has such a chance it is only handled by one person so that it becomes used to that person and not people in general. It does not see anyone else; it is kept away from everyone and everything that is unnatural to it. If it can be cured within twenty days and taken back to the spot where it was found, where its own territory is, then that creature has the best chance of survival. Beyond twenty days it is too late: often its territory will have been occupied by something else; what is more, the creature will have begun to adapt its behaviour to the conditions in which it now finds itself. The animal then has to go through release pens, which takes a long time.

When the badger was brought in, we handled it very warily because we knew only too well how viciously badgers can bite: once they have gripped something they will not open their mouths again before they have torn at it. We heard the car stop and saw the vet coming up the hill carrying a sack which might have held half a ton of gold. He is generally a neat, calm person: this time he looked very harassed: his hair was ruffled and his tie was askew. John went out to meet him.

'I don't want another morning like that,' the vet gasped, putting the sack down and collapsing in the nearest chair. 'There's a badger in there. I've sedated it so it's pretty quiet at the moment, but it hasn't half led me a dance. Two Alsatian dogs had it cornered in some bushes up on the golf course. It's got some quite deep cuts on it but there's nothing seriously wrong with it. A few days' rest should see it all right.'

'It's a funny time of the day for a badger to be about,' John said.

'Yes, I wondered if a car had knocked it during the night and left it dazed. It's near the road there. You've no idea the crowd that had collected up there. People with sticks were lashing into it and trying to get it out. If they'd only called the dogs off and let it alone it would have been all right, but people don't seem to have any sense where wild animals are concerned. The thing was in a frantic condition. It was snapping out at anything that moved; I couldn't leave it there – not in a public place like that.'

We can go years without seeing a badger and then we may have four or five of them at the same time. It was exactly the case this time: this badger made the fifth. Next to the house is the old stable block and the stable itself has a heavy stone floor. In general, when animals are brought in we put them in the stable until we can make other arrangements for them. Our first badger arrived with a broken leg; two others were tame ones which people had reared and had sent to us for release. A few days later a family had drawn up in their car, opened the boot and presented us with a big box containing a fourth. I could not decide whether it was unconscious or simply asleep; I suppose that the fact that it was snoring should have aroused my suspicions: unconscious things do not snore. The visitors told us that they had found it at the side of the road in that condition. Then they had simply put it in the box and brought it to us. We carried the box round to the stable. It was so heavy that it needed three of us to carry it. There was six stone of badger there – it was a very muscular animal.

The people asked if they could see the owls. They next asked to see a heron. In all, it must have been half an hour before they left. I went straight back to see to the animal. It had disappeared. There was only the one with the bad leg sitting in the trough at the end. In the middle of the stable was a pile of earth which reached halfway to the roof. The box which the badger had been in was completely buried and I thought the badger must be under all that rubble. I should have known better. When I had scrabbled enough earth away to reveal the box I could see that it was quite empty. So was the stable.

There was no doubt where the three badgers had gone. There was a hole in the far corner where the stones had been torn out. Who would have thought that three badgers could have moved so much soil in such a short time? What was more, they had carried on digging. Every day I had to go and move wheel-barrow loads of soil; every day John complained more and more about the effect that it must be having on the foundations of the house.

We simply could not entice those badgers out. We fitted up contraptions which would fall and trap them when they came out. They stayed where they were on those days. We left the doors open, but they preferred to stay where they were and dig in a bit deeper. Eventually they moved out. They have now taken over the rabbit warren in the copse.

Meanwhile, we had this new badger to look after. John had opened the sack and reached in for the badger, talking to it all the time. It was a big boar, and it growled when John first touched it. After a little while it seemed to understand that he was trying to help it and allowed itself to be lifted out without any trouble at all. Having done that, he did not know where to put it.

We always plan to have an empty cage ready, but things never work out like that. In fact, I cannot remember when we had one without an occupant. At the time of this badger's arrival, we had reached the stage where there was not a single empty room in the house either. We had to think quickly. The badger seemed amenable enough, but it was a wild animal and there was no knowing when it was going to turn and take a bite out of us. Then we had a brain-wave. We were keeping some young kestrels in the outside toilet. We gathered them up, and put them in the bathroom, and made a temporary home for the badger in the toilet. Two years later we had a letter from someone who asked whether it was true that we kept kestrels in the bathroom and badgers in the toilet. Such things do happen from time to time ...

The badger only spent a short time in his new home. By the afternoon of the same day we had built a run which we usually keep in sections and had installed him in that. I do not think we have ever had an adult wild animal which settled down as quickly as that one. It ate what we gave it and took its antibiotics without a murmur. It allowed John to examine the cuts on its head – although it growled as though to warn him not to take any liberties ...

The cut on his head was very deep. He must have

been dealt a blow that would have killed any other animal. Badgers in this respect are lucky: they have a double cranium and a blow on the head has little effect on them.

Badgers are wonderful animals. In some ways they are remote, yet they are completely self-assured. Being creatures of the night they have very weak sight. I doubt whether they can see more than six feet. Their acute hearing and strong sense of smell more than compensate for this deficiency. As long as they are left alone they are passive, harmless creatures, but if something worries them, they can turn and be really vicious. They are predators but they do not set out to kill – not like a fox. However, if something crosses their path, such as a rabbit, they will pounce and take it. If they come across a rabbit burrow, they will dig it out. In general, they will eat anything. They will dig out and feed on bulbs and roots. They are partial to insects, birds and eggs. A badger on a keepered beat can be a real nuisance. They love honey and they have a nose that will lead them straight to a bees' nest. Despite the size of their feet, they will clear the earth away so carefully that the whole untouched nest is exposed. It is wonderful to watch them.

They are meticulously clean, too. A badger sett has several entrances but you will know straight away if a particular sett is in use: there will not be a leaf or twig on it; not a hint of untidiness. They never make a mess in the sett – not like foxes. You only have to put your nose near the entrance to a fox's dwelling to know that one is in residence. Badgers, on the other hand, use a hole outside the sett as a toilet, and when it is full they dig out another. I know an old sett where so many of these toilet holes had been made that they made a complete circle round the mound. When the two lines met up, the badgers moved on to another sett. They often do move on for a week or two and will go visiting other badger families or dig out other holes and use those for a while. During their breeding times their habits change: they become as territory conscious as any other animal.

The badger does not have any real enemies except man. The Scots were a threat to them at one time because the traditional sporran was made from a badger's head.

Our badger stayed with us for three weeks. We did not take any risks with him. John looked after him and the children were told to keep well away from his run. One Sunday, a man who must have seen John feeding and talking to the badger called with some friends who were staying with him. We normally do not invite anyone in on a Sunday: it is our family day. St John called out to say that they had arrived, but John was out and I was doing the washing. I asked St John if he could keep him talking for a little while. Moments later, St John was shouting and calling out. I ran out with soap suds halfway up my arm. The arm was standing near the badger run and the door was open. The badger had hold of him by the arm and, while I was looking, he shook it as if it were a useless piece of rag. The man was holding on to the side of the run, trying to pull his arm out of the badger's mouth. The more he tried to pull back, the tighter became the animal's grip. I shouted to the man to let his arm go limp and then twist it out suddenly. He did not seem to understand what I was saying. He was shouting and kicking out at the animal as though it were his fault. I ran across and cut the badger with the side of my hand on the top of his nose. He loosened his grip straight away. I pulled his top jaw up and twisted the man's arm out of the way. He had been pulling backwards with all his might. When the badger's grip eased he tumbled to the ground.

I think the badger would have come at him again but I put my foot in the way. He trundled back into his run, shaking his head, sneezing and growling from time to time. I had hurt him when I hit him on the nose: it is a badger's most vulnerable spot. I looked at my own hand then: it was covered with blood. I realized that it was from the man's arm.

The man was sitting on the ground, trying to cover up his arm. He was swearing and complaining how wrong it was for people to keep dangerous animals in their gardens without putting notices up. I asked him to let me look at his arm but he said he could look after it himself. I thought he ought to see a doctor as quickly as possible. The whole sleeve of his jacket had been shred into three long strips. His shirt was torn, too, and I could see blood welling out from the gouges in his arm.

'Whatever made you take them over to the badger?' I asked St John.

'I didn't, they were over there when I went out. I asked him to come away. I could see the badger didn't like him. It was pacing up and down. He promised that he wouldn't worry it but he refused to move, and began telling the people that were with him about it. I was coming back to tell you when he opened the door. I ran back and told him not to but he said he was all right with animals and turned his back on me. Then he bent down and reached out to it. He must have been trying to stroke it.'

St John was upset – and so was the badger. In the three weeks it had been with us, it had accepted captivity, and had learnt that we were trying to help it. It would wander out from its sleeping box when we were in the garden and sit in its run, looking all the time to see what we were doing. When it was satisfied it would go back into its sleeping box. Every so often it would look round the corner to make sure that we were still there. It takes weeks, perhaps months to build up a trusting relationship of the kind which John had with that badger. Many people who own dogs or cats have done exactly the same, and the animal will never behave in exactly the same way with anyone else. If people can build up a trust like this with a domestic animal, you can imagine how much more delicate it is with a wild animal.

The badger never settled down again in the run. If anyone entered the garden it would crouch on the straw and growl, a really menacing sound which started in the base of its throat.

The time had almost come for its release. The cuts on its head had almost healed. We could not decide which was the best way to let it go. I thought that we should simply leave its door open because the golf course on which it had been found was not more than six miles away as the crow flies, and badgers have a well-developed homing instinct. We moved a number from an established sett when an area was being dug up for road building; they had found their way back in three days, a distance of over fifty miles in all. John disagreed. The badger had turned vicious and he was not sure that it would not try to attack some of the other animals in the centre.

'As soon as it feels there aren't any restrictions,' I

said, 'that animal will be as far away from here as it can go.'

John was still not convinced. He wondered whether we ought not to build a proper release pen near the place where it had been found. The principal difficulty would be that of keeping the public away.

That night the badger started to pace. He walked up and down, up and down the length of his pen. It is something we hate to see, and so we cleared all the birds away and opened the door. John went out the next morning to tidy up the run. A little black nose peeped out of the sleeping box. The badger was still there, and over the next few days it became clear that he meant to stay. We put his food outside the run so that he had to go out. Once or twice we caught sight of him ambling round the garden; we even saw him going through the gate over the fields, but when we went out in the morning, he would be back in his box. This continued for weeks.

We finally asked a lady who lived in the village if we could use her garage. We carried the sleeping box down and put it in the back of the garage and, after a lot of coaxing and poking, managed to get the badger into a sack. We took him down to the garage too, put him in his box, and put the food down in front of him. The badger settled down as quickly as he had done in the run in our garden. The next night he pushed the door open and he disappeared. We thought that the badger had gone for good, and was now looking after himself.

At the same time every night we took food down and left it in front of the sleeping box; every morning the plate would be as clean as a whistle. We never saw the badger again, however, and we began to suspect that we were feeding all the stray cats in the neighbourhood. We stopped taking any food down.

At two o'clock the next morning we were woken up by someone banging on the door. When John looked out of the window, he saw the lady who had let us use her garage to release the badger. She was standing on the step, looking larger than ever in her voluminous nightdress.

'Please come quickly,' she said. 'The garden's full of pigs.'

The woman was nearly hysterical. We put our coats on and hurried back to her cottage. We could hear the noise before we reached the bottom of the hill. Besides the snorting, there was crashing and banging. I held on to John's hand: it all sounded so eerie in the middle of the night!

They were not pigs, but badgers – nine in all. They were rooting round that garage, sniffing, snorting and upsetting everything in their way. They were obviously bad tempered. They had turned up for their evening meal and found nothing there. The badger which had stayed with us was easy to recognize because there was a deep line across his head where the hair had not grown over the cut. It seemed that he had not completely returned to the wild, but was having the best of both worlds. What is more, he must have fetched all his friends to taste the food. Every night that the lady was woken up by the badgers in her garden we had to put food out for them. However, now that the noise had been identified she did not mind so much; in fact, she quite liked having them about and had all sorts of people coming up to watch them. Even a television crew spent a night in her lounge. They took a marvellous film of the badgers from her lounge window.

In November they just stopped coming. At this time of year they go into a state of semi-hibernation; they become much slower and quieter, and we guessed that this is what happened to these badgers. They did not return in the spring either. Although it had taken longer than we had expected, we assumed that the badger was now living his own life again and finding his own food.

CHAPTER TEN: The Little Owl

When you live with animals like we do, you have a wonderful chance of studying them at close quarters. We have an opportunity of understanding them in a way which must be unique. Of course, they do not behave like an animal does in the wild – but many of their characteristics are the same.

We have a great sense of achievement when an animal which has been badly injured is fit to be released again. But it is the young birds and animals which are brought in and have to be hand reared which give us most fun. There are all sorts of problems – diet and warmth, for example – but it is not the rearing that causes the greatest headaches: it is knowing how to teach them to look after themselves so that they can be released and take their place in their own natural environment. Each one has to be treated as an individual. I suppose they are like children: some learn quicker than others.

An animal's behaviour can be divided into three categories: that which is instinctive, that which is latent instinctive (develops instinctively later in its life) and that which is learned. Always what most surprises me with animals which we have reared is how much they have to be taught before they have any chance of surviving in the wild. You cannot, for example, rear a tawny owl, and conclude that when it is fully grown and looks like the wild ones it can be taken out into the country and left there. It will simply not survive. In addition to anything else, the wild owls that live in that particular territory are not going to accept an intruder; if that owl does not behave in a way which the wild birds find acceptable, they will attack it repeatedly and kill it. It is the same with a sparrow. A flock of wild sparrows will not accept another sparrow simply because it looks like them; it has to behave like them as well.

A bird like a cuckoo is easy to rear and release because all its behaviour is instinctive – but that is an exception. For example, it is instinctive for a bird to eat but it must be taught how to choose its food. If you watch young blackbirds following their parents you will see how meticulously the adult birds show their young how to find insects. Somehow we have to think of ways of taking over this job and, as I said, each of them has to be treated as an individual.

One of the easiest ways is to put an adult bird which has been injured with the fledglings. They will pick up habits from the older birds much more quickly than they will from me; but sometimes that technique can back-fire.

I had six young thrushes last year which did not develop any interest in searching for their own food. It seemed a better idea to put the food in a dish and hand it to them in that way. I was also looking after an adult blackbird at this time. I put the thrushes into a large cage with him and within three days they were all pecking food from the ground and taking the occasional worm. Then I had an adult thrush and he was put into the cage as well. Knowing that snails make up part of a thrush's diet, I put a number of snails in the aviary. Five of the young thrushes showed no interest in them at all and the sixth was scared stiff of them. Every time one of them moved, it flew up to the other end of the run, getting as far away from it as possible and calling out as if it was being murdered. The adult thrush loved the snails: he attacked them one after the other and by the end of the week all the fledglings were eating them as soon as I put them in, banging them correctly on the ground to remove the shell. They became so enthusiastic about it that they seemed to think that everything had to be banged on the ground to make it more palatable; stones, earth, in fact anything they could hold in their beaks was banged on the ground. They were still doing it after they had been freed.

The little owl we had in simply refused to learn to look after itself; perhaps it knew when it was well off. It had been an untidy-looking creature when it arrived. It could not have been more than three weeks old: its feathers were still forcing their way through the baby bird's greyish fluff, and the patches of fluff alternating with the shiny new feathers made him look rather moth-eaten. The man who brought him to us was upset at having to leave him. He had been taking his dog for a walk when it had cornered something on the heath, and when he hurried over to see why the dog was barking, he found a grey squirrel with this chick in its mouth. There was a hazel bush behind it with a rounded bole in the side of which was a hole. It was clear from the way in which the wood had been broken away and lay scattered on the ground, that the squirrel had forced its way in and found the young owls. There were two dead chicks lying on the ground in addition to the one which the squirrel was holding. Without thinking, the man seized a stick and lashed out at the animal. The squirrel dropped the young owl, ran across the grass and leapt up a tree, hotly pursued by the barking dog. It was then that the man saw that the owl was still alive. It was moving feebly. He had picked it up and taken it home.

He had not known at this time that it was an owl: it was merely a small, grey, fluffy chick as far as he was concerned. In fact, it was so small that the egg tooth, the small bone-like knob on the bend of its beak which it uses to cut its way out of the shell, was still in its place. The squirrel had bitten right through the chick's wing and so the man took it to the vet. The vet identified it, and advised him how to feed it. He explained, however, that it was difficult to rear a young bird in unnatural surroundings and even more so when it had been injured. It was unlikely that he would be able to cope with both these problems. In the teeth of all these difficulties, he managed to rear the bird and then began to build it an aviary in his garden.

Then the neighbours objected. There was a clause that no animals could be kept on the estate. Someone found a local bye-law which prohibited the keeping of owls in the town because of the noise they made. Over a hundred people signed a petition asking the council to prevent this man keeping the owl in his back garden. So he had brought it to us.

It seemed daft that anyone could object to such a creature as that little owl, but it is true that when they grow up they can make a dreadful noise. What is more, as they are in the habit of calling out all night long they can be a nuisance to the neighbours. The man was nearly in tears when he handed the bird over.

'I felt like fighting them,' he told us, 'but what's the

point? We've got to go on living there and it wouldn't be much fun for my wife if the neighbours really don't like owls.'

We explained to the man that if we kept the owl it would not remain in captivity, and that if and when we thought it was fit, we would try and release it. He was pleased to hear this news because that was what he wanted for the bird. The only trouble was that it was not what the bird wanted for itself.

It was still very young and, consequently, needed heat. As the man had got into the habit of feeding it every time it called out, I carried on in the same way. I found that it was easiest to keep the bird in a shopping basket and carry it round with me. I kept its food in a dish in the corner of the basket as well so that it was always ready. It only took that owl two days to dispense with my services altogether: when it was hungry, it ran across to the corner of the basket and helped itself. Within a very short space of time, it had developed a fixation about the basket I kept it in. It was only an ordinary shopping basket in which I had spilt a tin of paint, so I painted the whole thing green to improve its appearance. At first, the owlet had just peeped over the rim. I would be washing or doing the housework and get a sudden feeling that something was watching me. Sure enough that rather flat-topped round head would be peering over the basket's edge, turning this way and that to match every move I made. Birds cannot move their eyes and keep their heads still as we can: they have to change the position of their whole head if they want to look in a certain direction. Birds' eyes differ from ours in other ways too: they have both monocular and binocular vision; that is, they can bring both eyes forward and look at one thing (as we can) or they can use their eyes independently of each other, looking at two different things on either side of them at the same time.

Very soon that little owl had jumped on to the side of the basket and from there to the handle – although he would jump back into the basket quickly enough if there was a sudden movement or a noise he did not like, and bury his head under the newspaper with which I lined the basket. I suppose he thought we could not see him then.

He was the most inquisitive bird we have ever had. He wanted to know everything that went on; he did not like to be left out of a thing. He was like that before he got all his feathers. If, having perched himself on the edge of the basket, there was something he could not see very well, he would stretch out as tall as he could possibly go so that his whole body became long and thin; then he might suddenly bob down so that his head was tucked into his shoulders and he became short and round and fat. He did not look the same bird at all. When something really intrigued him, he would bob up and down like that ten or eleven times, one after the other; all the time his eyes would be fixed on whatever had captured his interest.

It was not long before he was running across the floor or flying round in the room after the things which intrigued him. He would bob his head up and down at them, turn one way and then the other as he studied them a little more carefully. If he was still puzzled, he would seize hold of the thing and pull it to pieces with his beak. I generally tuck my handkerchiefs up my sleeve – at least, I did until we had the little owl. Unfortunately, the piece of material poking out seemed to fascinate him and time after time I would find him sitting on the floor shredding my hankie into little pieces. Flowers were a constant source of fascination, and they received the most violent treatment of all. As he grew older I had to give up keeping potted plants altogether. After all, there is nothing attractive about a lot of shredded and chewed leaves and flower petals piled in a pot of earth – which is what my plants looked like after Little Owl had attacked them.

Things that intrigued him most were the ones that moved. When I dusted, he would fly and settle on the shelf or whatever I was dusting and try to catch hold of the cloth. We had a clock which ticked quite loudly every time the hand moved and Little Owl was fascinated with it. He spent ages with his beak pressed firmly against the glass. Whether he was trying to catch the hand – or simply adjust it back – I do not know. Sophie had a clockwork ladybird that ran across the floor when it was wound up, and turned round and round before it went on again. The owl was really puzzled by it. As soon as Sophie wound it up and put it on the floor, he would be down and running along beside it, his head getting nearer and nearer until it seemed that his beak was touching the key. When the ladybird started to turn, the key would hit the bird and the owl would jump back as if it was scalded. Gradually he would move nearer and nearer again until the whole pattern was repeated again. After a while he would turn his back on the clockwork ladybird and pretend he was not interested in it at all. Seconds later, his curiosity having got the better of him, he would turn and chase it across the floor again.

At six weeks, Little Owl was fully grown and fully fledged. He was a pert little bird, stood straight up on his two feet, and looked interested in everything. He was quite small – approximately six inches long – and a mottled greyish brown in colour. His breast was pale. The pale ring of feathers which encircled his head and gave him a disc-shaped face came to a point at the top of his beak, which made him look as though he was permanently frowning. His eyes were bright yellow and alert. In the wild, little owls are crepuscular: they are not purely nocturnal creatures like other owls, but will fly both day and night. Little Owl was much more interested in running round the house than flying. He never walked: he was always in a hurry. As soon as there was a noise or a movement in the room, he would scurry across to find out what was happening. He moved about so silently that we would often not realize that he was there. It would give me a shock to reach out for the teapot and have a little owl bob its head over the top at me when I thought he was back in the lounge with the children. St John found it a bit disconcerting, too, to have the owl pop its head out from behind a pile of books when he was doing his homework. It was probably the movement of St John's pen which had fascinated the bird.

The vicar had a bit of a shock one day. He had called and I had made him a cup of coffee. He was sitting in the armchair stirring the drink and, as he often did, he went on and on stirring while he talked. That was too much for the little owl. He flew up on to the arm of the chair, ran along it and peered at the spoon, his head getting closer and closer to it until the two were almost touching. When the vicar looked down and saw the owl there, he jumped out of the chair as if he had been scalded. We nearly were too: the cup flew up into the air and we all had a bit of his drink.

We fed Little Owl on meat which was red raw. We

had added the calcium and vitamins which he needed and he ate those without any trouble; but, being an owl, he needed to eat a certain amount of roughage: fur or feather, for example. In the wild he would have eaten the whole insect or animal and brought up the matter he could not digest in the form of a neat little pellet about eight hours later. For the few days that we had fed him by hand, we simply put small pieces of string or bits of sheep's wool with his food and he had swallowed the lot. Now that he was feeding himself, however, he would have none of it. Lean steak and chicken were his favourites: he did not want anything else. We tried putting the pieces of roughage round each little bit of meat but he was not going to be tricked. He would either unfasten it and eat the chicken in the middle or he would leave it altogether and take a piece of meat which had not been covered.

We tried to get him interested in insects. In the wild, little owls eat a lot of insects; our little owl showed no interest in them at all – not as food anyway. It was Sophie's job to go out and find beetles and centipedes each morning. Unfortunately, as soon as she had brought the insects in, she began to feel sorry for them. She would run round and try to collect them and take them back to the garden before Little Owl caught them. She need not have bothered: Little Owl did not understand that he was supposed to eat them. He would run across the room and study them by bending down so close that his beak was almost touching them. But when they continued to walk across the room at the same pace, he lost interest and ran off to find something a bit more exciting. Much to my annoyance, by the time the children gathered them up again some of them would have disappeared. One evening I was sitting watching television when a stag beetle walked right over my foot!

Little Owl did eat some insects – but only by mistake. He was fascinated by the flies which buzzed in the window, and would spend ages running up and down the window sills chasing them. He could not understand them at all. One day he caught a Daddy Longlegs. He had been watching it for a long time, bobbing his head up and down to get a better view of it and turning his head right round so that he could study it at a different angle. When it still took no notice of him he grabbed it with his talons and stood there with the insect weaving helpless patterns in the air with its long legs. He did not know what to do with it. He turned his head first on this side and then on the other to look at it. When its legs continued to move, he bent down and caught hold of it with his beak – and then it disappeared. He had swallowed it. After that he often ate flies which he caught in the window, but he never searched for them. He gobbled them up because he simply did not know what else to do with them.

St John decided to teach him to recognize worms. He dug up half a dozen and put them on the kitchen floor in front of the owl. The bird did not know what to make of them at all. He ran up and looked at them, bent his head down so he was looking at them a bit more seriously, bent his head down further so that his beak was touching them, and when the worms continued to unwind themselves and glide steadily across the floor without taking any notice of him, he turned his back on them and pretended he was not interested in them at all. His curiosity got the better of him and he was soon turning his head round to look at them again. Then he would run after them. At this point the biggest worm of them all turned and started to travel towards him. Little Owl jumped right up into the air and down again when he saw that. When the worm continued to come steadily on the bird decided that he did not like worms at all. He flew up into his basket and scurried under the newspaper so that they could not find him.

Little Owl had a fixation about shopping bags and baskets of all kinds. I suppose it was my fault for having brought him up in that green painted basket.

The baker from the next village called twice a week. He baked his own bread and brought it to us in a large old basket. He had not been gone more than a few minutes one day, when I heard him come back into the kitchen. He dropped his basket on the floor.

'Look at that,' he said as if he could not believe it himself. 'Look at that.'

I looked at the basket and saw nothing out of the ordinary.

'I was getting this loaf out for old Mrs Jones when a head popped out from under it. Gave me quite a turn it did.'

I looked at the basket again. A small round head with bright yellow eyes peeped out from behind the bread, looked at me for a couple of seconds, and went back again.

'Owly,' I said sharply. Little Owl flew out and up on to the window sill. Turning his back on us, he stared out of the window as if what had happened at old Mrs Jones' house had had nothing to do with him at all.

My friend Gertrude generally popped in for a cup of tea each afternoon. She always carried a huge bag with her wherever she went. It weighed a ton and we never could decide what she kept in it. We were always too polite to ask.

Little Owl was not. As soon as she sat down and dropped her bag on the ground beside her, that bird would be in it, popping its head out from time to time and having a look round to make sure the rest of us were still about. Gertrude was too busy talking to notice him. When she did realize she had an owl in her bag, she would tell it off as if it were a naughty child. When it heard her voice, the owl would tunnel to the bottom of the bag and hide. That was how we found out what Gertrude carried round with her: she had to empty everything out to find the bird. She found her front door keys which she had lost weeks before; she even found some cheese sandwiches which were so hard that they must have been there for months. In addition, out came papers, make-up, pens and, last of all, Little Owl. Gertrude took him home twice. She only realized he was there because she heard scrabbling in the bottom of her bag.

He liked to get in to anything dark. If a cupboard door had been left open, Little Owl would fly in to investigate. A box was even better. One day he got into the teapot. I did not know he was there until I reached out for it and his head bobbed out of the hole. The hole he liked the best was the one left in the bedclothes when I was in bed, where the clothes left a gap near my back. Little Owl would scrabble down this and lie down beside me as if he thought he should have a proper bed and bedclothes. I was always afraid that I would turn over and squash him – but he was cunning. He only came into the bedroom when the alarm went off. I could sleep through the alarm any day but an owl scrabbling down the bed and settling down in the small of my back was enough to rouse anyone.

Anyone who met our little owl would not have imagined what killers they can be in the wild. They can clear all the song birds in a copse. There was not a small bird left in the trees near one family of young owls – only a family of wrens which nested in the same hazel tree. The owls did not touch them. Owls can be vicious to others of their kind, too. One night we watched a pair of little owls driving some tawny owls from their territory. They attacked and fought each other as viciously as any animal I have ever seen.

Our little owl was the one exception: there was nothing spiteful or vicious about him. He was friendly and interested in everyone and everything, and would run up to investigate any new arrival which was brought in. I suspect, however, that it did small birds like thrushes no good to have an inquisitive owl peeping in at them. He enjoyed the company of the children, and we encouraged him to follow them outside in the hope that he would spend more and more time out of doors. He was not too keen on the idea. It was all right for a time – but he soon wanted to come back indoors. If the door was shut, he would sit on the window sill and bang on the glass with his beak until we let him in. He had a favourite window at the bottom of the stairs whose ventilator we left open all the time so that he could go in and out at whim. He soon learned where it was. We would often go out in the garden and find that the owl was flying after us. It would sit on our shoulders or follow us round from tree to tree.

Sometimes he would go and sit on a perch next to one of the hawks or buzzards. Any of them could have killed him: they were much bigger and stronger than he was. We chased him off every time that this happened, but he never seemed to appreciate danger. Once he sat in the middle of the road while a lorry went right over him. Fortunately, the wheels passed on either side of him and he was not hurt. He had not had the sense to get out of the way. When the combine harvester was going round the fields in the autumn, Little Owl would fly across and investigate the corn coming out from the chute and on one occasion was almost buried alive in it. Luckily one of the men saw what was happening and stopped the machinery. The owl flew back to the cottage, screeching.

This is one of the things which worries us about creatures that are reared in captivity. How can they be taught that some things are dangerous? Most of them have an inbuilt suspicion of objects which make a noise or move suddenly. In these particular cases, however, the owl had been intrigued and, rather than get away from them, he had tried to find out as much as possible. We tried to frighten him away from the road and make him understand that cats and dogs should be avoided. There seemed to be so much to teach him all the time. We tried to persuade him to stay outside longer but, as soon as it showed the first sign of rain, he would be back through his window.

One day the weather had turned suddenly cold and John shut the window without thinking. Finding that he could not get in, Little Owl had simply searched for another window that was open – and that happened to be one in our neighbour's house. It was about ten o'clock when we heard the screaming. Mrs Cook had gone to bed and the owl had decided to get in with her. I think the whole village must have wondered what had happened.

We tried to make it learn that it had to catch its

food before it could eat it. John tied some meat to a piece of fur which looked a bit like a mouse and dragged it across the floor. That provided fine sport for a few minutes but the owl soon tired of it. We persevered by refusing to feed it but pointing to the meat attached to the fur. Little Owl became really cross with us. If we were not going to give him food when he demanded, he would have to go and look for his own. The problem was that food to him meant something red. He would simply search for anything red and try to eat it.

He found a beetroot first. The maroon stains down the kitchen wall are evidence of that escapade. The front of his face was stained red as well, and I suppose that he had eaten a bit and hidden the rest of it for a later date. I was finding bits of beetroot for days. He had mainly hidden it behind cups and dishes on the shelf, but there was one piece draped artistically over the lampshade and another on top of the potted plant. The bird must have sneaked some into the lounge as well: when Gertrude called that day and sat in the armchair, she must have found another piece of beetroot that the owl had hidden. When she stood up and turned round we saw that she had a purple behind. All told, we had little success in persuading the owl to go wild.

It was during the winter that we had another little owl brought in. This one was a hen bird. It was not until we saw the two owls together that we realized how small our own bird was in comparison. Amongst birds of prey it is usual for the cock bird to be smaller than the hen, and our two were strikingly different in size. The hen looked twice as large as the cock.

This owl had been picked up at the side of the road

with a broken wing. We had it set and kept the owl in a box to keep it quiet. Unfortunately, the owl had a mind of its own and refused to stay in the box. I called it Houdini: it could get out of anything. Half the time I could not see how it had escaped. It seemed to be able to worm its way through a gap that was barely an inch wide. Considering that it had one wing strapped tightly to its body, it was amazing how that bird could get round. At first our owl was suspicious of this new arrival; but by the second day he was prepared to go up and look at her; by the third day they were almost inseparable.

I was nearly a nervous wreck by the end of those three weeks. I never knew when and where those two owls were going to appear. Several times I reached up to get a cup from the shelf and was so startled by two owls' heads popping out from either side of it that I dropped the thing and smashed it. They both had this habit of appearing suddenly when I least expected them.

It was fascinating to see how the behaviour of our tame bird changed now that it had another for company. The hen seemed neither tame nor wild. It was tolerant of us and completely self-assured. If we were in the room, it would hide and stay absolutely still. If we sat motionless and she forgot we were there she would run out and move round just like our own bird. Soon our owl developed the same habit: rather than flying over to us and running across the floor to investigate the children's games, he would retire behind a chair or stay very quiet until he thought that he was alone. We fed the new bird on day-old chicks and our own bird changed to this diet within days. This made feeding much easier: a chick contains all the goodness which a bird could need as well as the fluff which birds of prey require for their roughage.

On the twentieth day we took the plaster off the wild bird's wing. It had set beautifully, although it was a little stiff. Normally we would have taken this bird back to the place where it had been found, but by this time the two owls were inseparable. They settled the issue themselves. The ventilator in the hall had been left open. The next I knew, both owls were sitting in the apple tree in the garden. When I went out they both flew away and I knew that they had gone.

I told John when he came home. We felt a bit sad. Little Owl was such a character we knew we would miss him. I went in to make a cup of tea, reached up for the tea caddy and two owl heads peeped out, one from each side. I dropped the tea all over the floor. For the next couple of weeks I dropped lots of things on the floor because those owls kept appearing and disappearing until I thought they would drive me mad. Gradually they came indoors less and less. Eventually, the hen bird always waited out in the garden. The trouble was that it was our neighbour's garden and not ours. Mrs Cook was terrified of the bird after her experience in the bedroom. She kept coming and asking me to take it away, but by this time I had no influence with the bird. It was completely wild again. When I tried to drive it away, it simply returned to the same bush in her garden.

Our little owl rarely ate the food we provided now. When we broke open the pellets which we found on the window sill we found the remains of beetles in them, which was a sure indication that he was coping for himself. One day the two owls simply disappeared. That summer a pair of little owls reared five young in the old hollow ash tree not a hundred yards from the back door. We like to think they were the two that had been with us. Unfortunately, they used to appear and disappear so often that we had neither rung them or put a spot of dye on their feathers, and so we had no means of identifying them for sure.

CHAPTER ELEVEN: The Bittern

Life would be a lot easier if we could plan a week or even a day ahead – but things rarely work out like that. When we get up in the morning we never know whether or not something unexpected is going to happen; in fact, it is unusual for us not to be involved in something unusual as a result of our interest in wildlife. The trouble is that problems never seem to turn up singly. We may go weeks without being asked to take an animal in, and then there may come a week when the phone never stops ringing. It was like that the day the bittern arrived.

We were still living in Hampshire at this time and, because John was away on business, I had to cope with both the animals he generally looks after and my own. In addition to this the telephone had not stopped ringing all day and several animals had been brought in, all of them seeming to need a lot of attention. So when the man phoned up and said he had a bittern in his kitchen, I was a little bit short with him. First, bitterns had become rare in the part of the county where he lived (they had at one time been so common in certain parts of Hampshire that a suburb of Southampton had been given the name 'Bitterne'). Secondly, if it was a bittern, it was unlikely to be sitting passively in the corner of his room. The man insisted there was nothing seriously wrong with it; that it was simply not very lively. His description of it certainly matched that of a bittern.

He had found it at the side of the road, had taken it home, and had then not known what to do with it. I advised him straight away that if it was a bittern he must be very careful how he handled it, and that if he had children he should keep them all away from it.

'There's no worry about that,' he said. 'It's ever so tame. It lets the children go right up to it and stroke it. It's not a bit bothered. It doesn't even mind when they pick it up.'

There is generally only one reason why a wild bird behaves in that way: it is too sick to object. I explained to the man that bitterns can stab out with their beaks, causing untold damage, and that he should be very careful with it. I then told him to put it in a cardboard box, and to keep it warm and quiet. I would come and fetch it. Unfortunately, the man did not have a car so I had no choice but to get the car out and go and collect it myself. I would have liked to have left it until the morning – it was by this time very late – but the bird was probably too sick to be left that long. I woke up the two children (who were by this time in bed), bundled them into sleeping bags and drove off to fetch the bittern.

That poor bird: it was lying on its side in a slatted chicken box on top of a bed of straw. I thought that it was dead until I leaned down and heard its laboured breathing. In addition to anything else, it had pneumonia. It was after one o'clock when we got home and as soon as I had settled the children back in their beds, I took the bittern from its box. When I picked it up, I knew that it was beyond hope.

It was so light that it did not feel like a bird in my

hand at all. There are several things one looks for in a healthy bird and the bittern had none of them. A healthy bird crosses its wings tightly over its back when it stands, its eyes are bright and the feathers are firm on its head. Most of all it is the thickness of flesh around its breast bone which is indicative of its general condition. The breast bone of this bird was so sharp that it felt like a skeleton. It had no flesh on it at all. When a bird reaches that condition there is nothing one can do to help it. Yet I could not leave the bird to die.

Its first requirement was warmth. I put it carefully into a cardboard box next to the heater. As I lowered him in, he threw a fit. He threshed about in that box in what I imagined were his death throes; but then the rigidity left his body and I could hear his laboured breathing again. I could at least treat the pneumonia. I fetched the antibiotic and, mixing it with some food, warm milk, glucose and Complan, drew it into a syringe and squirted it down the back of his throat. The bird did not have the strength to object. Slipping my fingers round his neck, I slid them downwards and felt the liquid going down. It was a funny feeling: like forcing water down a hose pipe.

I gave him three syringes of food and was just getting ready for bed myself when the phone rang. It was John. He was worried because he had been trying to phone me all evening and I had not answered. I told him about the bittern and gave him my opinion that the bird stood little chance of surviving. It was too sick and weak.

I set the alarm and got up each hour during the night. On every occasion I gave him the same amount of food. The next night I reduced its feeds to every two hours and by the end of the week I was feeding it at three-hourly intervals. In spite of the fact that I stopped adding the antibiotic after the third day I still gave it the same liquid food. By the end of the week all sign of the pneumonia had disappeared. The bird, however, was still very sick; it continued to lie on its side and every time I looked into the box and saw that it was still breathing, I breathed a sigh of surprised relief. That went on for ten days. Whoever got up first in the morning was asked, 'Is the bittern still alive?'

We would not have been surprised if the answer had been in the negative. What surprised us still more was his tenacious hold on life: his simple refusal to die. We never were able to decide what exactly had been the matter with him. There was no sign of any injury. We wondered whether he had been poisoned. His droppings in the first few days had been bright green – which showed that his stomach was empty; in addition, there was an odd sickly smell to them which made us suspect poison.

On the tenth day, Sophie came into the kitchen when I was peeling the potatoes and said simply, 'The bittern's gone.' I was not really surprised but I was disappointed to think it had been holding on to life for ten days and when we were thinking that it was going to live after all, it had died.

'No, it's not *dead*,' Sophie said in exasperation when I told her how I felt. 'I don't mean that. It's not there. It's gone!' 'Gone where?' 'We don't know but we can't find it anywhere.'

I followed her into the lounge. As soon as she opened the door, I saw the bird. It was sitting on the back of the settee, as motionless as a statue. Its beak was pointing firmly towards the ceiling and it was balancing on one leg. The other one was tucked up under its body.

'Oh!' exclaimed Sophie. 'We didn't look there. We were looking on the floor.'

We put him back in his box and shut the lid. As soon as we left the room again, he climbed out and assumed his statuesque position on the back of the settee. By the time we returned to the room, however, he would be lying in his box, head drooped, beak on the floor, looking as sick as a bird at death's door; if we left the room again for a second, he would be out of that box. But how did we find him out? Well, one day...

We decided to catch him out. Birds cannot count. We all went into the lounge and a few minutes later St John and Sophie walked out again, making a lot of noise. It sounded as if we were all leaving the room. John and I waited there without moving, watching the box. Sure enough, as soon as the door shut behind them, a long green toe fixed itself firmly over the edge of the cardboard box. This was followed, slowly and steadily, by the rest of the bittern. With the same easy, steady movement he took another single step – and he was on the floor. He moved across the room in the same smooth rhythm.

There was something about the way he moved which made us want to laugh. To start with, bitterns are not the most attractive of British birds. You can see immediately how closely related they are to the heron; but this bird seemed even longer and thinner. Everything about it was long and thin. It was a mottled brown in colour and when you looked at its markings carefully you could see how delicately the patterns blended. It had a long, thin neck and a long, thin, sharp, greenish-yellow bill. But the feature which we noticed first was its long, yellow-greenish legs and its long, thin toes. It stood well over two feet high and most of that height was leg.

We had never seen a bird move quite like this before. It would delicately lift up one leg, circle it behind, bring it up in the air, and finally lower it softly to the ground. Then it would bring its other leg forward in a similar huge circular sweep. As he moved, his head came down and forward so regularly that you would have thought he worked by clockwork. He did not seem to walk so much as move forward in a weird, loose-limbed way. There was no variety in his speed and no jerkiness in his movement – just this steady, forward flow. Because his legs were so long, he crossed our lounge, which was eighteen feet long, in three strides.

His destination was obvious: he was making for that same spot on the back of the settee. He lifted his foot with the same circular movement, planted his three long toes firmly on the chair and, instead of walking forwards, simply rose up forward with the same easy movement. Then he tucked his foot under his body, pointed his beak towards the ceiling and settled down for the day.

Once he had got into that position he would stay like it for hours at a time. Nothing would disturb him. The children could play, shout and bring their friends in: the bittern would not budge. He stayed so still that visitors who came either did not realize that he was there or thought he was stuffed. They noticed the smell though. There was nothing we could do to hide that. Being a fish-eating bird, he gave off a strong, pungent smell and it seemed to get everywhere. I had added minced fish and chicken to his diet by this time, but I still had to force-feed him, easing the food right down the length of his neck. We could not persuade him to feed himself.

His diet was still liquid – and so were the messes he made. Fortunately, he was very much a creature of habit and liked to sit in exactly the same place each day, so I could cover the floor round him with layers of newspaper. In spite of the fact that he was much fitter than when he had arrived, he was still a sick bird and, consequently, still needed heat. This meant that we had to keep him near the heater in the lounge. The mess and the smell were becoming so overwhelming that I was looking forward to the day when we could wean him from the heat and into the open air. The bittern accelerated matters of his own accord.

Not only had he taken over the settee, but he began to object to anyone else sitting there. It was Gertrude who got it in the neck – literally on this occasion. She had sat down and dumped her huge bag on the ground beside her without noticing the bittern who was seated behind her in his usual beak-to-the-ceiling pose. Before she could even begin her first sentence the bird moved into action, bringing its long leg slowly forward and settling it on top of Gertrude's head so that his two long toes drooped over her forehead like a fringe. He then brought the rest of himself forward and, tucking his other leg up beneath his body, looked as though he was set for the day. I have never before or since seen Gertrude at a loss for words. She went scarlet in the face when we started to laugh. There is rather a lot of Gertrude – except that it usually goes sideways rather than up and gives an impression of roundness. If you add to this a long-legged bittern perched on top of her head, you can imagine that she looked very odd indeed.

I went round and picked the bird up. I suppose that by habit more than anything else I slipped two fingers over the back of its neck. It was a good job I did: he suddenly stabbed out. It was so rapid and unexpected that I did not have time to get out of the way. He cut me right across my cheek. If I had not restricted him by holding his neck, I think that he would have caught my eye.

It was a warning. He had let us know that he could be nasty and I warned the children to be careful in future. I need scarcely have bothered. Having been brought up among wild creatures, they have developed an affinity with animals which both John and I envy. This was much more marked when they were younger. We have often looked after animals which have been almost impossible to handle, yet they have gone to the children with no trouble at all. Two badgers, in particular, I will always remember. They were so vicious that we simply could not get near them. Yet when St John approached them, they ran up to him and followed him round as if he was one of their own kind. It was the same with the bittern. He would always be seated on the back of the settee when the children were in the lounge, and each would be aware that the other was present. But did they take any notice of each other? Not a bit. When friends visited, however, the bittern reacted differently. He would come down from his perch and, in his slow moving, circular gait, walk towards them so quietly that they did not even notice him. When he was near enough, he would stab out at the visitor and then, in the same steady movement return to his place on the settee. He did not stab hard; it was more like a warning. Unfortunately, the children did not know this and when they saw him coming, they would run. Hearing shouts and screams, I would rush in to see what was the matter. The visitors would be dashing round and round the furniture pursued at his usual leisurely pace by the bittern.

We made his box stronger, but he refused to be kept in. He managed to ease himself through the narrowest gap and in time we became used to a bittern skulking round the house.

Then one night there was the most dreadful noise. It sounded as if a foghorn was sounding right outside the bedroom window.

'What are you doing, Mum?' Sophie shouted.

I do not know why they thought I might be the source of such a weird noise.

Then it came again; a vibrating boom that echoed and re-echoed through the cottage. The bittern was booming. They say that you can hear them three miles away when they boom out on the marshes – so you can guess what it sounded like when the bird was in the next room to us. The noise settled the matter of its sex, though: only the males make that noise and then only at mating times. If I had been the prospective mate I would have been driven away rather than attracted by that din. John got up and turned on the light, which quietened him down for a bit. Unfortunately, now that he had found his voice he seemed to want us all to know: as soon as we got back to sleep, he started up again. So John got up and banished the bird to the bathroom.

We would have moved the bittern there before but it was already full of guillemots which had been oiled. We do not aim to fill the house with sick birds, but when we are looking after some which need to be kept warm we do not have much choice. We put the bittern in a small pen against the airing cupboard (a very warm spot). We had no idea how he would behave towards the other birds. We attached very high sides to the pen so that he could not get out. As usual, we underestimated the length of his legs. He simply stretched them a bit further and eased himself out in exactly the same way he had done in the lounge. Only this time he chose to perch on the hot water tap. We became so used to his being there, that we did not take any notice of him. The bittern even refused to get off his perch when we wanted hot water, and one day Sophie tried to turn the bittern round instead of the tap.

At first we had wondered how he would behave towards the other birds in the room – but we need not have worried. The bird seemed to remain completely aloof from everyone and everything. He spent most of the day sitting there with his beak in the air as if everything which surrounded him was beneath his dignity.

The only time he really came to life was when the oiled birds had their baths. He would then step down from his perch in one long stride and get into the water with them; but once there he would resume his same statuesque, beak-to-the-ceiling pose. Although he *seemed* very aloof, he would never miss what was going on. When we threw sprats into the water for the guillemots, he reached out, seized them, and had swallowed them whole before the auks had a chance.

That was the last straw. For five weeks we had been force-feeding him. Our fingers had been getting sorer and sorer as time went on because the bittern had got into the habit of waiting until our fingers were in his beak and then shutting it tightly. The edge of his beak was very sharp! We had tried all kinds of tricks to persuade him to feed of his own accord and none of them had worked. But as soon as he saw the other birds eating, he would decide to tuck in with them. And once started, he never seemed to stop. We began to think that our supply of sprats would never last. He soon discovered that there were sprats in the boxes and pens where the oiled birds were kept – in addition to the ones in the bath at bath time. So at regular intervals, he would take a circuit of the bathroom, moving at the same steady speed into each pen in turn, stepping up and over each partition without any difficulty. He would eat every single fish that he could find.

It was about this time that the photographer came to see if we were keeping any unusual birds. In general, we dislike journalists poking about, but this man was from the local paper. He often called in if they were short of a story: the bittern was just up his street. He set his camera up in the corner of the bathroom, positioned his lights and arranged all his other equipment. Space being a bit short in there, we shut the door and left him by himself.

We never discovered what exactly had happened. Suddenly the door burst open and the photographer dashed out of the house and down the road as fast as his legs would carry him. He would not come back into the garden let alone go into the bathroom again. He even refused to come in to say goodbye – but he gave St John some money to go and retrieve his camera and equipment.

Now that the bittern was feeding normally, we thought that it was time for his release. Unfortunately, things did not prove as simple as they seemed. The landowner who let us release water birds on his land refused to have the bittern there. They are such poachers and do so much damage to the fish that he did not want it. The people who had found the bittern in the first place had kept in touch with us, and they found a marshy area where we were allowed to let the bird go. After being in captivity for three months it would need time to adapt to the wild again. We discovered, however, that it was not practicable for us to erect a pen on this stretch of marsh. Instead, I had to accustom it to a pen in the centre. We made a collapsible run and at exactly the same time each day, his food was put out in a dish. Within a week he seemed to have accepted both his feeding time and his surroundings and I arranged to meet the people who had agreed to release him down at the marsh. That bittern departed in the same aloof way that we had seen in our home – but I suppose we should have expected it. The actual release point that had been chosen looked to be approximately a mile from the road, and struggling across that marsh with the sections of his pen was a job I did not want to repeat. We finally had it in position and I went back to fetch the bird. The couple who were actually releasing the bird had laid in a supply of sprats. They put some in the dish for him. I put the bittern in the pen and we stood back and watched. For a few seconds nothing happened at all. Then one long leg appeared through the doorway; the rest of him soon followed at the same measured pace. The bittern moved steadily forward through the long grass in exactly the same way it had roamed round our lounge. There was a fence a few yards from us. When he reached it, he simply lifted up his foot and placing it over the top bar, flowed over at the same steady speed.

Then we watched him as he walked steadily on through the rushes and long marsh grass. If it had not been for his purple tail, we would not have been able to see him at all; his markings were such that he merged completely with the grasses through which he was walking. (I must explain I had not meant to give him a purple tail. I had wanted to put a marking on his tail so that we could recognize him again, but I had pressed the plunger a bit too hard.) He went on walking until he was lost from view.

Nobody ever saw him again. The lady continued to put fish out for him at the same time every day but they were not taken. Of a hundred birds released during those three months, that bittern was one of only six that did not return to the spot from which it was released within the first twenty-four hours. As it was impossible to keep a constant watch on the place, we could not be sure that it had not returned in our absence.

The following spring, bitterns nested on that marsh; the first recorded time for thirty years. We wondered if one of the parents was ours, but we could not be sure. The local bird watchers, however, thought that they had detected a trace of purple . . . I spent some time in the marsh trying to catch a glimpse of it, but to no avail. I can't grumble though. John and I were given a grand dinner for helping the bittern to return to that area and we hope it is the progeny of our bittern that still visit the Meon Valley.

CHAPTER TWELVE: The Swift

Sometimes people phone us up and tell us excitedly that they have picked up a really exotic bird. Generally speaking, when we are told that we are going to receive a hobby, a merlin or even an eagle we can be pretty sure that a cuckoo will turn up. Many people tend to look up the more unusual birds when they are trying to identify the one which they have seen; they look disappointed when we explain that it is only a common cuckoo.

'We've picked up a bird. There's nothing wrong with it that we can see. The only problem is that it can't stand and won't try to fly.'

We receive calls of this kind every summer without fail. We know before we set eyes on the bird that it will be a swift. Swifts can be difficult to identify in the hand because they bear no resemblance to the sleek arrows they become when in flight. People will often bring in a swift and stubbornly insist that it is something completely different.

One day a man phoned to tell us that he had found an osprey with a broken leg, and that he was going to bring it over. He was absolutely adamant that he had identified it correctly. We awaited its arrival with mixed feelings. Ospreys are wonderful birds but they are very expensive to keep in such a centre as ours as they feed on freshwater fish. We could already see the bills for trout that were likely to come in ... Our suspicions grew when a car drew up outside and a man climbed out carrying a container that was little larger than a shoe box. His wife followed him into the kitchen and, putting the box on the table they carefully lifted the lid to show us the osprey. Sitting on some tissue paper in the corner of the box, watching us with its dark, beady eyes, was a swift. We tried to explain to this couple that it was in fact a swift, and that it was much too small to be a bird of prey. We told them that you measure an osprey in feet and a swift in inches – there is that much difference in their size. The two old people refused to be convinced. What is more, there was nothing wrong with the bird. Having landed on the ground, it had found it difficult to get back into the air.

This couple had obviously not believed us because they later made a statement to the press about the osprey with a broken leg. We knew that something must have happened because people started calling and requesting to see the rare bird or take a photo of the osprey. When we told them we did not have one, they looked at us very strangely. I am sure that most of them thought we were lying. If they had read in the paper that we had a sick osprey at the centre, then we must have one. We even had somebody turn up from an animal society who thought that we should hand such a rare specimen over to him. He did not want to hear about swifts – he had come for the osprey. I know that he did not believe us because he sat there repeating, 'If what you tell me is true ...'

The trouble was that the very same couple played a similar trick on us the following year: only this time they brought us a sick moorhen and announced to the press that they had found an eagle.

I think that it might have helped the first time if we had kept the swift as evidence, but as soon as the couple had driven off we had taken the bird across the fields and let it go. It takes a swift a little time before it rises. There is a mile long, straight road, which runs along the top of the cliff between Hough-on-the-Hill and Caythorpe. St John used to love cycling along it to school when he was smaller because he said it made him feel that he was going along the top of the world. The great width of the Trent valley is spread out like a patchwork carpet reaching out to Lincoln and Newark; before the farmer obstructed the view at one end of the road with a conglomeration of modern farm buildings, you could clearly see the shadow of Boston Stump from there.

We launched the swift from one end of this road, and then drove along it to keep the bird in sight. We consider that it requires a full mile before it has begun to fly strongly. Sometimes we have to go and pick up swifts that we have released there and push them up into the air again; sometimes they plummet to the ground before they get the full force of the air beneath their wings which enables them to lift up towards the sky.

Once they are airborne they stay in the air for the rest of their lives. They never return to land again except to nest. They eat, sleep, mate and hunt solely on the wing. Swifts are birds of the summer: they soar and turn, float and dive, dark aerial arrows against a backcloth of the summer sky. Swifts are to the land what shearwaters are to the sea: masters of the air. Yet they are clumsy and awkward on the ground. They are often mistaken for swallows or martins because they migrate to Africa in the same way and they have a similar long-winged appearance in the sky. But the wings of a swift sweep back like a scimitar and their manner of flying is much more direct and powerful. They are dark-hued birds, brown-black in colour with the exception of a white patch about the throat. They have shallowly-forked tails, but the impression they give is of dark shadows wheeling across the sky.

Some country folk call them devil birds. If any of them land on the ground, they will not go near them because they associate their dark shapes with evil. But it is really their weird, long drawn-out screams filling the air which have earned them that name, particularly when the young birds are flying with their parents. The softness of a summer's evening will often be disturbed by groups of swifts screaming and calling as they swoop and swerve through the sky. They build clay nests on the sides of buildings or on cliffs. The entrance hole is in the side. You can often see the parent bird clinging by the edge of this hole. Their legs are set well back on their bodies so that they can easily perch in this sideways manner.

Once they are on the ground though, they are stuck. Their legs are too far back to give them any lift, and they cannot launch themselves into the air from a flat surface. They will shuffle round, however, at an amazing pace. One lady brought a young swift over to us that she had found walking down Sleaford High Street. She said she had passed it earlier as she walked along the main road two miles outside the town and was sure it was the same bird. She was probably right. It had certainly walked a long way: its legs and feet were red raw from the unaccustomed exercise, and we had to give it a three-day course of antibiotics to prevent infection before we took it back to the fields and lifted it into the air. Once they are airborne their shuffling gait disappears immediately and they become creatures of perfect symmetry and power.

When people phone us about a swift which has grounded, we explain how it has to be helped into flight, telling the people how the palm of the hand holding the bird must be kept flat and that it must be brought sideways through the air in a slicing movement so that the birds are obliged to spread their wings to keep their balance. Then – and only then – will they begin to fly. We rarely have a second call.

On this occasion, however, it was different. I think I must have made the whole thing sound too simple to the lady on the phone. She had let her little girl take the swift into the garden and throw it into the air. The child, having grasped it too tightly, had thrown it to the ground and broken its wing. Now it was lying on the ground and they did not know what to do. I went over straightaway. The wing looked bad at first because it had been twisted right round – but it was not as bad as it appeared at first sight. It was a clean, simple fracture and we managed to strap the wing firmly into place without any difficulty.

We knew, however, that to get that swift back to the skies was going to be a race against time. The wild swifts were already gathering in groups in readiness for migration. Some of the groups were so large that small, swirling clouds seemed to sweep across the sky as the swifts flew together. Birds need three weeks to mend a broken wing and we had to be sure that this swift's wing would be strong enough to carry it to Africa.

John prepared the cage for the swift. He had draped old jumpers up the sides and over the perches. The swift loved it. We wasted hours watching that bird climb round and round its cage like a tiny mountaineer.

As leopards are the escapists of the animal world so is the swift among birds. And that small bird which we kept out in the kitchen was no exception. It seemed to be able to undo the most complicated catch with its long, almost prehensile feet. We would be sitting watching the television thinking the swift was safely shut up in its cage for the night when we would catch sight of something moving across the carpet. At first we wondered whatever it was: it moved in such a peculiar way, its wings outstretched, its head reaching forward close to the ground, and swaying irregularly from side to side.

The swift developed the habit of appearing unexpectedly. As we were eating a meal he would crawl up over our shoulders or climb into our laps. We had visitors one day and the lady did nothing but talk and talk. No one else could get a word in edgeways. Then she looked at the chair opposite her and her speech became slower and slower until she was not talking at all. She was staring at this chair as if she had seen a ghost.

'What is it?' she asked timorously.

The swift was climbing up over the back of the chair and moving round in the same way as it did in its cage. When you saw it like that it did not look like a bird at all – certainly not the swift which one associates with such speed and power in the air.

The swift liked to cling to our jumpers most of all. He would attach himself to our chests and stay there for hours on end. Once a man who called at the house thought that I was wearing a peculiar kind of brooch and was quite shocked when it started to move.

The swift not only liked climbing up things: he enjoyed getting beneath them as well. One day I was sitting reading and I felt something crawling round in my underclothes. I felt about me and eventually found – that swift! It must have climbed up over my shoulder and down under my collar. He was always turning up in the most unexpected places. We nearly sat on him several times because we had not seen him on a chair.

Then one day he completely disappeared. We searched and searched. In the end we sadly decided that he must have got outside and been caught by something like a cat. When I got into bed, I felt something crawl over my legs. I jumped out of bed a lot quicker than I had got in! There was the swift, weaving its haphazard route across the bedclothes.

If it had not been for his penetrating call, we would have lost him altogether many times. But he was always hungry, and when hungry he would shriek out for food. He was no trouble to feed. At first we had put the food in his beak. That was easy: swifts have such a huge gape for their size! In the wild, they fly round with their mouths open, taking in insects as they go. Soon our bird would reach out for the food when we held it out. He would try almost anything – but his favourite dish was meal worms. He would have lived on those if given the chance. Meal worms on their own, however, would have proved far too rich a diet, and would have killed him. He tolerated maggots and ate chicken without any trouble. We had no difficulty in keeping his weight steady. That is the trouble with small birds: if they begin to fade and lose weight, you can do practically nothing to bring them back to peak condition.

It really was a race against time with that swift. Before he had been with us a week, we watched the wild birds congregating and beginning to fly off. Birds, like swifts, have such a strong urge to migrate that if they are thwarted, they will often simply lie down and die. A swift's reaction can be even more complicated. It can go into a very deep coma – like a form of hibernation. It seems to sink in and out of these coma-like trances very quickly.

That was what happened to our swift. Its temperature dropped suddenly during the night. I went in to see how the bird was doing, and found it flat out on the bottom of the cage. It had died in the night – or so I thought. Rather sadly, I brought the body in and laid it on the draining board. Normally I would have taken it outside but we were keeping a check on broken wings at that time, and I wanted to see how this one was mending. We had breakfast and after that I made the beds. The swift was out of my mind for a couple of hours. When I went into the kitchen the bird, to my great surprise, came crawling over the rug towards me, screaming as if it had not been fed for days. It clambered up my arm and settled on my shoulder, snuggling into the warmth of my jumper as it often did.

In the next few weeks, it went into deep comas three times. On one occasion it stayed like that for twenty-four hours. If I had not seen what had happened that first time I would have probably taken the swift across to the shed and left it there. But now I waited for him to come round. He would always be starving when he did wake up.

We took the strapping off his wing on the twentieth day. It had mended beautifully. Normally we keep the birds for a couple of days after the strapping has been removed in case the wing is not as fit as it seems. But we could not allow the swift that length of time. All the previous week John and I had been noting the movement of the swifts over the valley. We had plotted where they tended to congregate and over which fields they could generally be found. They seemed to range for miles as we watched them through the binoculars. It was difficult to keep track of them because swifts are renowned for their fast, powerful flight; and when they are in a group these attributes seemed to intensify. They swept across the sky, a cloud of living movement, constantly changing shape within the group so that from a distance they looked like wisps of smoke being tossed this way and that by the wind. It was the speed with which they moved that fascinated us. They were congregating and moving on. One moment the sky was empty of them; the next, another group of birds arrived and began to grow in numbers again. These must have been the last to depart: we had been noting that the groups were growing smaller in size. The birds which were leaving England now were those that had hatched late in the summer.

As I came home from work on the day that we had taken the strapping from the swift's wing, I saw a group of swifts gathering above the hill where they always seemed to collect. I stopped and watched them for a while. Then I realized that the pattern of their flight was changing: they were circling, gaining height. Then they were moving over a wider and wider area in a steady circular movement, and I knew that they would shortly be moving on. I hurried back to the cottage and fetched our swift. I was in such a hurry that I did not even wait to take it out of its cage. When I got back to the hill, the sky was empty: there was not a swift to be seen. That afternoon I went round to all the places where the birds could generally be found. I saw plenty of swallows dipping over the mill ponds and martins collecting insects for their late broods, but there was not a sign of the dark-feathered arrowheads for which I was looking. So the swift came back home again. He was not worried. He clambered all over his woollen slopes and seemed delighted to be back.

We spent hours looking for swifts in the next few days but we did not see one. We knew then that we had left it too late: they had all gone. It was no good letting our bird go on its own. They need the protection of the group for the journey and our swift, having been in captivity for those weeks, needed it more than the others. It had to relearn the habits of the wild ones, and the only way to do this was to be with them. Migratory birds released on their own do not survive.

We would have put a plan in action that we had used before: to have the bird sent out to Southern Spain and released by an acquaintance of ours who had helped us in this way before. We got in touch with the airline and asked them to inform us if someone would agree to take it. In the past, we had carried the bird in a box to the airport, and handed it over to somebody on the plane. They in turn would hand it over to the person who was waiting to meet them in Spain.

I shall never forget one middle-aged lady who helped us out like this. She did not attempt to hide her feelings that she was having the best of the bargain: John collected her from her home and took her to the airport. When she arrived in Gibraltar, she was met by the man who was collecting the bird. He drove her to her hotel. On occasions there was a bird to bring back as well, so we made the same arrangements for meeting her when she returned home. When John mentioned casually that there were martins to be taken out and an *eagle* to be brought back, I thought that she would faint.

One of the airline staff offered to take the swift. We were waiting to hear from our friend that he could meet the plane but, as it turned out, we did not need to use them after all.

It was the day the vicar had called. I do not think he likes coming to our house very much. It always seems that he arrives in the middle of one emergency or another or gets himself into some peculiar situation – like the time that he nearly sat on the fox cub or the other occasion when the kestrel sat on his head and made a mess right down the back of his neck. He had just sat down with his cup of coffee when the door burst open and John rushed across the room shouting: 'There are swifts on the hill! There are swifts on the hill!'

Seizing the bird's cage he rushed out again before I realized what was happening. I would have liked to have seen that little bird go but I did not have the chance.

John later said that he did not think it was going to make it at first. He had tossed it into the air and the bird had flown round and round without gaining any height. Then the swifts above it started to scream and dipped lower in the sky and our little bird circled higher towards them. Soon they were all flying together. John watched for a while but when he turned to come home he said that he could not say which was the bird that had spent the month with us. It was quite indistinguishable from the others.

CHAPTER THIRTEEN: The Lapwing

There is a quality about wild animals which I find fascinating. I love to watch wild birds and animals moving freely in their own environment; seeing how they live and listening to the sounds they make. John and I have spent nights out of doors watching the rutting deer, or sitting beside worn badger paths so that we can see how they behave away from their setts. We have camped out in the Scottish hills watching and noting the peregrines; we often spend a day watching the geese on the Wash. I do not think we intrude in any way: I like to think that we are sharing their world, even if it is only for a short while. It is the same with the animals which come into the centre for care. We share their lives for a short time and, if everything works out well, we have the chance of watching what must be the ultimate in animal care: the return of a creature to its own natural environment.

As a family, we have spent some of our happiest times out in the countryside, watching the birds and animals. One of the birds I never tire of watching is the lapwing, that long-legged regal bird with the delicate wisp of feather on its head, giving it a slender crest. It is a dark bird: and from a distance its plumage looks black, but when you get nearer you can see that these dark feathers are shot with green and purple; when the light catches them from different angles they seem to be constantly changing colour. The pure white cheeks and underparts, the orange-brown colouring beneath the base of the tail, make a beautiful contrast with the darker feathers.

For me, lapwings represent everything that is noble in the countryside: the freedom and beauty, the vastness and the seclusion. They are one of the most common British birds found in the country, and they live on the moors and in the big open fields. You can often see flocks of them on a freshly ploughed field or following the plough with their slow yet powerful wingbeats. When you see them flying, you realize how they earned the name of lapwing: they really do seem to lap the air. They may seem heavy birds in the air with their wide rounded wings, but their flight is powerful and graceful. Their wings come down low beneath their bodies as they fly. They twist and turn, spiral and dive with unexpected grace. I am sure that lapwings fly simply for pleasure: they tumble through the air, crossing and recrossing the horizon with the same beautiful flight. They fly together, whether it be in small groups of maybe half a dozen birds, or in huge flocks which sweep across the sky like a small cloud. They always fly in complete unison, swerving and turning at exactly the same time, following no particular leader but always moving together. They change the speed of their flight in the same way, switching from the almost static, fluttering, butterfly-like flight to the sweeping direct movement across a valley in the same instant. We have tried for hours to catch sight of one moving before the others but it never seems to happen: they move in complete unison. When you have several hundred birds in a single flock moving in this way across the sky, it is a fantastic sight.

Lots of people call lapwings peewits because of the noise they make. Their high-pitched call seems to call out the name 'peewit' – although to me it sounds more like a squeaky toy. When they pair up in the spring, their long drawn-out calls echo and re-echo across the fields and moors and sound very eerie. Their correct name is the green plover, but most country folk call them lapwings. A farmer down the road has even insisted that they are called 'pyewipes'!

On the ground they are different birds altogether, running forward on their long thin legs for a few steps before they pause and then run forward again. They weave their way through sheep and cattle as they search for insects, stepping out daintily and graceful, yet with a hesitance which makes me think of them as the gazelles of the animal world. They seem busy, active birds on the ground, but they are always alert. If anything unusual approaches, they lift into the air immediately, moving together, as if called by some kind of telepathy, flying off with their slow, steady, distinctive wingbeats.

It is very unusual for us not to have a lapwing at the centre. We can always reckon on having certain creatures here: foxes or badgers, tawny owls and kestrels, thrushes and magpies and, of course, a lapwing.

Main roads attract them – particularly the verges of motorways. The steady vibration of the traffic draws the earthworms to the surface providing an easy meal for the plovers. When they are out in the meadows, you can watch lapwings stamping, moving their feet up and down so regularly that you can hum a tune in rhythm with their movement. This stamping bring the worms to the surface. The bird must feel when a worm is about to surface because it will dive at the ground and, more often than not, stand up again with a wriggling meal in its beak. Some lapwings have found that traffic will do the job for them: they do not have to stamp at all. Whether they have lost the ability to do so or simply do not bother with it any more I do not know, but lapwings which are brought in from the main roads rarely stamp on the turfs as do those which are brought in from the open country.

We live near one of the oldest main roads in the country, the old Great North Road or the A1 as it is popularly known. The AA man often brings us injured birds which he has found on the road and nine times out of ten they will be lapwings. They are not run over in the normal way; in fact they hardly ever venture on to the hard surface of the road. Most often, they will have been sucked in by the air current which is set up by heavy lorries and injured in that way.

The lapwing I will always remember had also been picked up at the side of the road – but it had not been injured in the usual way. A friend mentioned it casually to me one afternoon.

'I meant to tell you a couple of days ago,' she said, 'but the people down the road from us have this bird that's hurt itself. They asked whether you would go in and tell them how to feed it.'

She did not know anything else about it – not even what sort of bird it was, or whether it was still alive. If it had been found hurt two days ago, and they had only just decided that they did not know how to feed it, I doubted very much whether it would still be with them now. To my surprise, it was: just.

The lady took me down the garden and showed me the lapwing. It was lying in a rabbit hutch on some straw. It did not have the strength to stand. Its eyes were shut and, if it had not been for the heavy, laboured breathing, I would have thought it dead.

I looked at the bird and did not know what to say. The family had obviously done their best for it. There was a bowl of bread and milk and a dish of water near it, but that lapwing was much too weak even to notice. It lay on the straw near to death; even its crest drooped limp and lifeless beside it. It was one of the most dejected and pathetic creatures I have ever seen.

The young lad who had found the bird by the side of the road walked up just then. He was eleven. That bird meant a lot to him.

'There were birds all the way along the grass,' he said. 'Most of them were gulls but there were a few lapwings as well. This was the only one alive. It tried to run away when I picked it up and nearly went under a car, but I caught it. It couldn't run straight, you see – not with a wing as badly broken as that. So I put it in my saddle-bag and brought it home.'

This lapwing had been shot. There was no doubt about that. I stretched its wing out. The neat hole through the shattered bone was unmistakable. I later checked up on the dead birds which the boy had described to me. They had all been shot. I took some of the bodies to the police. They knew all about it.

'They go along in these cars, shooting at anything that moves,' the sergeant told me. 'Highway cowboys, we call 'em. There's no sense to it. Try and catch them and prove it, it's another thing altogether.'

That was what had happened to this lapwing. It was a victim of those 'highway cowboys'.

'I took it to the vet's and he wanted to put it to sleep,' the boy had continued, 'but I couldn't have that so I brought it home. He told me to try it on bread and milk. I've put plenty of fresh food in but it hasn't touched a thing.'

The boy wanted to keep the bird himself and he was prepared to do everything I said. I explained how it had to be kept in a constant temperature. He insisted he could have it in his bedroom. I told him that it must have antibiotics and saline to counteract the effect of the loss of so much blood. I explained how the wound must be cleaned and the wing strapped up. The boy listened to everything. He was determined to care for the bird himself. His mother rather settled the matter by refusing to have it indoors. While the two of them argued I looked at the lapwing and thought it did not stand a chance now whatever happened to it. It was so thin and light that it did not feel like a bird in my hand at all. Even while I looked, its eyes seemed to glaze over. I thought that it was dying.

Then the boy's mother began to explain to me that the house was not big enough for the boy to bring his animals indoors. He would fill the house with animals if he could. And even if he did bring in a bird, the cat would get it. She would much rather I took it away with me.

So I took the bird home. I felt really guilty about it because I knew how much the lad had wanted to care for it himself, although I doubted that he could have saved it. Now it had to get better. If it did not, I would have felt that I had let the boy down.

The bird was pathetically thin and too weak even to swallow any food I put in its beak. By easing a tube down into its crop, I managed to get some saline solution and antibiotics into it. Then I put it in a warm spot and left it quiet.

For three days I kept it on saline, adding a little egg yolk and Complan to its antibiotics. It was given this every two hours throughout the day. On the third day I could no longer hear its laboured breathing when I approached the box. I thought that it had died. Mercifully, it was still alive, although it was still too weak to stand or lift its head. At least the antibiotics had cleared the infection from its lungs.

We had strapped up the bird's wing when we had brought it home. We had done it quickly because we did not want to shock the bird more than was absolutely necessary; what is more, it had been three days without attention so it was doubtful whether it would mend properly. Now that the bird was not merely hanging on to life but struggling to recover its health, we wished we had taken a little more care with the strapping.

For two weeks we kept him quiet and in the warmth. He was so weak that I would not have been surprised to have found him dead at any time. We had kept a dish of water in the box with him. It was not that we thought he would be strong enough to drink: we wanted to prevent dehydration by keeping the air moist. For the first few days he had a hot water bottle near him in addition to the heater, which kept the temperature at a constant seventy-five degrees. If the water had not been present, exposure to that amount of heat could have caused complete dehydration, brain damage and even paralysis. We fed him all the time by intubation: a length of bicycle-valve rubber which we eased down into his crop. He was fed on Complan, egg yolk and a little glucose. This diet provided enough nutrition but did not increase his weight. I had tried him with raw red meat, but he did not have the strength to swallow it.

To our amazement, that lapwing's recovery was as sudden as it was complete. I was sitting reading the paper one afternoon when I heard the sound of water. I went and checked the taps and looked round outside but everything seemed all right. I went back indoors and sat down again. I could still hear water.

It was the lapwing. It took me a long time to realize. When I looked in his box, not only was the lapwing standing up but he was splashing and washing in the dish of water, looking very pleased with himself. From then on, he seemed to have decided that he had had enough of that box. As soon as I opened it, he would jump out and walk round the lounge as if he owned it. If the dog dared to move or someone came into the room, the bird called out with its long drawn-out, haunting note. For an instant the country seemed to have come into our lounge.

Now that he was stronger, I could give him a more natural diet. I cut pieces of meat into the shape of maggots and put them into his beak. He swallowed them without any trouble at all. The only drawback was that, however we tried to tempt him, we could not persuade him to pick up food for himself. I brought turfs in and scattered food on those but he did not even look at it. I bought meal worms and maggots but he turned his back on them. I dug up worms by the dozen and put them in dishes of water. He deigned to go up and look at them, and even turned his head on one side to get a better view, but he would not bend down and pick one up, let alone eat it. So I had to force-feed him.

We left him without food for a whole day thinking he would eat quickly enough when he became really hungry. The food remained untouched at the end of the day.

'You'll have to be hard with that bird,' John said. 'It never will eat if it's got you putting the food into its beak for it.'

I was hard unintentionally. We had been out for the day and arrived back very late. When I got round to looking at the lapwing, his dish was clean: he had eaten every scrap of food I had put out for him. From then on, feeding was no difficulty – as long as I put out enough. Now that he had started eating, he always seemed to be hungry.

Although the wing had set much better than we had expected, it was dropped – although not badly enough to prevent it flying. We thought that it would pull up once it started to exercise it.

That lapwing was such a happy little bird. He trotted round the house, tried to peck the pattern off the carpet and moved round so quietly that we often did not notice he was there until he suddenly ran across the room or disturbed the peace with his wailing note. In general, he would wail when he came face to face with something he did not like, generally the dog. The poor animal nearly became a nervous wreck trying to avoid the bird. The lapwing was equally happy outside. When we transferred him to the outside run he settled down as quickly as he had done indoors. The only trouble was that he would look so miserable when we went indoors last thing at night, leaving him outside on his own, that I generally gave way and brought him back in with me.

John said we were making a fool of the bird: I suppose we were really. The thing was that that bird gave me a feeling of personal pleasure. You see, the boy who had found it had been cycling over regularly to see how it was getting on – a journey of about twenty-four miles. That pathetic creature had meant so much to that boy that it simply had to get better. Sometimes I wondered whether he had willed that bird to live.

He came out with me when we took the lapwing out across the fields. Lapwings seem such friendly birds. They spend so much time together that you would think that all one would have to do is to introduce ours to others of its species and they would be pleased to welcome it. Unfortunately, it does not work out like that. Although they are not territory conscious in the same way that robins and owls are, they are still very jealous of their own positions within the flock, and at nesting time they will guard their nest area with a ferocity that seems completely out of character with the placid long-legged bird which had been running round our lounge. It is very important that the wild birds approach the one that is being introduced to them rather than the other way round. If they sense that a strange bird is coming too close, they will become suspicious and fly off, leaving the new bird completely isolated. Or if it is the time of the year when they are pairing, they may attack it.

We put the bird in an adjoining field so that they could hear each other. For a couple of days, they may well ignore a single bird but, sooner or later, they will fly across and spend a while with him before returning to their own field. They may do this two or three times a day and for several days on end. As they gradually become used to each other, their calls change slightly and the bird we have introduced flies back with the wild birds. Each night, for a long time, it will return to the field from which it was freed. We have one bird that comes back every evening (in the winter) to exactly the same spot where we let it go five years ago. Even if the boys are playing football there, that lapwing will settle down in the middle of them.

I did not expect this bird to be any different from any of the others. I explained to the boy how he must expect the birds to react as he walked across the field with me. I took the lapwing out of its box and put it on the grass. It ran around and started pulling worms out of the ground straight away. We watched it for a while and then walked back to the cottage. It was when I was going through the gate that I saw something move out of the corner of my eye. I swung round and – there was the lapwing, following neatly to heel.

We took it back again and again. In the weeks that followed, I must have taken that bird out and let it go about thirty times. On every occasion it followed me home as if I had trained it to walk to heel. I started playing hide and seek with it, lifting it out of the box and hiding behind the hedge so that it could not see me. But whatever tricks I played on him, that bird would be right behind me when I walked through the cottage gate.

I had no reason to believe that it had flown back to me: it could walk as fast as I could run! John began to think that I was bringing it back on purpose. He insisted that I must be hard on it – or it would still be with us when the wild birds migrated! We always have lapwings here throughout the year but they are never the same birds. In the autumn they migrate a little further south and return in the spring just before the swallows arrive. Lapwings we have marked on release have appeared in Scotland in the summer – which means that they must have migrated about three hundred miles. This bird needed to go further south for the winter. I knew that I must get it flying in the next ten days if it was to be strong enough on the wing to fly. There was no reason why it should not take to the air: its wing was quite fit. We had to provide the stimulus that would make it want to fly, and it was finding the right kind of stimulus that was the problem. Generally the wind and the fresh air is enough, but this bird wanted more. There was only one thing for it: I had to force it upwards. We were not keen to do this because it can frighten the bird, and if it shows difficulty in flying, it may be hard to restore its confidence.

I recruited a dozen children to come home with me after school. We spread out in a long line across the field with the lapwing in front of us. At a given signal we all ran forward shouting for about four metres and then stopped. When I gave the signal we went forward again, driving the bird in front of us. We went up and down the field. The lapwing kept spreading his wings as it ran, but it still kept its feet firmly on terra firma. Then suddenly it was flying. It was just as well; I do not think I could have run another step! At first he only flew a few feet before settling on the ground again. And then as the children went on, he flew a little more, and then a little more still until he was actually flying: circling, soaring, seeming to play in the air. The dropped wing looked more noticeable now that he was airborne but it did not seem to slow him down. Even as we watched, his flight seemed to grow stronger, and as he flew he started to make a similar sound to the one that had haunted our lounge during these last few weeks. Only now it really *was* the call of the wild.

I stood there watching the bird until St John said,

'Mum, look at those people over there.' It was then that I saw the two ladies standing near the gate. One of them was much shorter than the other, so short in fact that her chin only just cleared the hawthorn hedge. I did not find out until later that she was actually the taller of the two. Unfortunately, in her enthusiasm to come and tell me what she thought of me, she had failed to negotiate the ditch. The other woman was shouting too and waving an umbrella at me. I went over, wondering what was upsetting them. It turned out that I was. I suppose that to take a group of children out to chase a lapwing across a ploughed field is a rather peculiar pastime. They did not give me a chance to explain what we had been doing. They simply stood there and shouted. One of the women tried to emphasize her argument by waving her umbrella. Unfortunately it kept unrolling and getting in the way. All the same I stepped back because I really thought they were trying to stab me with the thing. I was quite pleased that there was a hedge between us. I tried to explain what we had been doing and I think the older of the two began to listen, but they were determined to have the last word.

'Well,' said the lady who was still half in the ditch, 'if the poor bird doesn't want to go, you've no right to make it.'

Turning on their heels, the two of them marched off up the hill using their umbrellas as walking sticks, and refusing to get out of the way for anything – even the car that was trying to edge past them.

Meanwhile, our lapwing was doing well. I was able to watch it a lot that next week because its dropped wing made it easy to distinguish. I saw it on one flight and heard it calling. I soon realized that its calls were being answered and, as I watched, a group of seven lapwings flew up and round our bird. When they settled on the ploughed earth, our bird sat with them. That night it was back on its own in the field where the two old ladies had shouted at me but, during the following days, it spent more and more time with the other lapwings until I could no longer distinguish it on the ground. It was only in the air that I could identify it. When the others left the fields that autumn, our lapwing went too.

CHAPTER FOURTEEN: The Hedgehog

We receive more daft telephone calls about hedgehogs than anything else. There must be more hedgehogs than almost any other animal in this country, yet there are not many people who seem to know much about them.

One woman who constantly phones up bought a house with an acre of walled garden. She decided to fill it with hedgehogs. I thought for a time that she meant china ones. She took offence when I sent someone round to see her who makes plastic hedgehogs, gnomes and windmills as garden ornaments.

When I appreciated that she was going round the countryside collecting wild hedgehogs for her garden, I was speechless. I tried to explain that hedgehogs have their own territories and habits – as do many other animals – and that if you put large numbers of them together it upsets their patterns of behaviour. I also explained that an acre could only provide enough natural food for four or five of them. She insisted then that she would feed them herself. I tried to explain that if they came to rely on unnatural food they would no longer be wild animals. It all ended well enough. Having found out how much was involved, she spent a week redistributing her hedgehogs. Not that it is ever difficult to find somewhere to release hedgehogs: gardeners will always take them and at one time you could get a good price for them. Hedgehogs are particularly fond of the pests which gardeners most dislike. They will gobble down a slug as soon as it has the audacity to show its head.

Then there was the phone call which we received in the middle of the night. It was two o'clock to be exact. I answered it in a sleepy voice.

Someone was telling me that there was a hedgehog at the top of Beech Hill which was behaving in a peculiar fashion. She could not tell me why it was behaving peculiarly but she seemed very worried by the fact. I told her to bring it to us if she thought we could help it. Being unable to do that for some reason, she gave me detailed instructions of the exact spot where the hedgehog could be found.

John was awake by this time and wanted to know what was happening. When I told him about the hedgehog he said, 'They're drunk. Fancy phoning us up at this time in the morning!' and promptly turned over and went back to sleep.

I agreed and went back to bed myself – but I could not get back to sleep. I kept thinking of this hedgehog and wondering if there was something wrong with it. In the end I got into the car and drove out there to investigate.

It was a warm summer's night. Dawn was already breaking when I reached Beech Hill. The hedgehog was there, exactly where the lady had told me it would be. It was scrabbling up the bank. Unfortunately the ground was too steep for it to make any headway. Judging by the marks which had been scratched in the earth, the animal must have spent all the time since she had phoned trying to get off the road. If it had only gone a few feet to either side, it could have climbed on to the grass without any difficulty. I picked it up and put it there. It went straight back to the spot where I had found it and started to scrabble at the earth again. It did this three times. It did not attempt to roll up or scurry out of my way as I would have expected. I wondered whether it had been knocked by a car. Thinking that a couple of days rest would give it a chance to sort itself out, I put it in the boot and started off for home. At least I meant to start off for home. I could not get the car to start. I was in a real panic then because the night had been so warm that I had not put a coat on over my nightdress, and I did not want anyone to see me as I was. I got it started in the end and when I reached the cottage I ran a bath and got straight into it. I had hardly touched that hedgehog but I had been in contact with it long enough for its fleas to transfer themselves to me. I was covered with them. That is one of the troubles with hedgehogs: they are made in such a way that they cannot scratch themselves well enough to keep clean.

I was just beginning to feel clean again when John rattled the bathroom door. It was time to get up. While John was shaving I went out to fetch the hedgehog from the car boot. When I lifted it up, I started to shout. John came running out, his face only half shaved, to see what was the matter.

The hedgehog was lying there quietly. Beside it lay four tiny pink little objects. She had given birth in the car. John collected an armful of hay and put it in the gap in the hedge. I carried mother and babies carefully across to it and laid them gently down. Now I had to have another bath: I was covered in fleas again! By the time we came home from work, the hedgehog had rearranged the hay and the young animals were hidden from view. I was glad that I had found them: if she had stayed at that spot on the hill, I doubt whether any of the family would have survived.

As things turned out, it was us who scarcely survived. The noise every night was fantastic. It started with the dog. He objected to them being in the garden and, as soon as they started to move, began to bark. Even when we shut him up indoors he seemed to know they were roaming round the garden and barked and barked. The hedgehogs themselves were none too quiet either: those young ones squealed and called as if they had been fully grown pigs. All night long they carried on and none of us got a wink of sleep. I am relieved to say that over the coming days they roamed through a wider and wider area, and eventually disappeared.

A well-known lady phoned us up one day and asked if I could go down to see her. She had a problem. John took the message and when I got home he said that he thought I ought to go and see her because she had sounded upset. She was upset: when I arrived at her house she told me that she had lost her hedgehog. It seemed that she had a hedgehog living indoors. Noticing that the French windows were open I explained to her that it was only natural that it would want to go outside – and, what is more, that there was nothing to stop it. Perhaps it was as well if it did live in more natural surroundings. It would be better for the animal.

'You don't understand,' she said, 'and no one else knows. I brought it up. When it was tiny I used to keep it in bed with me so that it was warm. It usually sleeps with me every night except during the winter months. No one knows how much I miss it.'

'Sooner or later, it will want to go back to its own kind,' I replied.

'It never has before and it comes in at the same time for its milk every night. It's never missed a day and has never been late.'

'How long have you had it?' I asked.

'Nine years,' she said.

This sort of thing was a little outside my normal experience, but we sat down and worked out how that hedgehog normally behaved: which paths it normally took and at what times it did certain things. Hedgehogs are very much creatures of habit so that it was quite easy to build up a day-to-day pattern for it. The lady had a gardener who kept his tools in a brick-built outhouse.

There was an old fireplace in the corner and this was where the hedgehog slept in the winter. The gardener had bricked it up the week before, and it was then that the hedgehog had disappeared. We fetched him back from his tea and persuaded him (after much grumbling) to knock the bricks out. There, curled up on the dead leaves, was the hedgehog. Well, that was three years ago. The hedgehog still lives there, and shows no signs of old age.

More recently, we had a telephone call from a Mrs Boden. She had hand-reared a hedgehog from the day of its birth and she wanted to know if we would release it for her. I explained that it would be best if she could let it go in her own garden because the animal was familiar with its surroundings. If, in addition, it had freedom of movement, it would gradually go wild as it came into contact with the other hedgehogs in the garden. She did not want to do this because she was worried about a road nearby. Being out at work all day, she could not keep an eye on the hedgehog as she would have liked. What is more, she claimed that she could not understand the behaviour of the animal. She had taken a lot of trouble to seek someone who knew about hedgehogs but no one had been able to help her. To rear an animal like this was an achievement and, having got that far, she wanted to do what was best for it. If she had made a false move and the animal had died, she would have felt guilty ever after.

When she brought the animal to us she handed it over with very mixed feelings. She wanted the animal to go wild and yet she liked to know that it was safe. She had carried the hedgehog in a big cardboard egg box with a small hole in the side. This hole was no bigger than three square inches and I was amazed that the two-and-a-half pound animal could get through it. But it did – without any difficulty at all. Inside the box was the hedgehog's nest: an oval wall of hay, chewed up paper and dead leaves, all woven together so intricately that, however roughly we handled the box, the nest was not disturbed at all.

We kept the hedgehog in the mews. The agreement was that it would not be freed until it had become used to us. I put its food down at exactly the same time each evening and used the dishes which Mrs Boden had used. I had about a dozen kestrels in the mews at this time and they were being fed on day-old chicks. When they had eaten their fill, they dropped the rest of their food on to the ground. That hedgehog would be on to it straight away. He much preferred the chicks to the carefully cut cheese and meat, which I prepared for him.

Mrs Boden brought the hedgehog to us soon after it had come out of its winter sleep. It had weighed two pounds eight ounces when it had finally retired into its box and it weighed two pounds seven ounces when it was brought to us. That surprised me. I had always thought that these animals lived on the fat which they had stored and that they would therefore be much lighter when they finally awoke than they had been the previous autumn.

That hedgehog made us feel that we had to start learning about animals all over again. We have often looked after hedgehogs; in fact, we have treated them so casually that I have never bothered to note their arrival unless they had an unusual injury. Generally they are half grown animals that have been hit by cars and need a few days' rest before they amble off into the countryside again. This hedgehog was the first one that had been reared in captivity from such a young age. I did not expect him to be any more difficult than a fox or a stoat.

The first problem was that he would not go outside. I put his box out on the grass and he would not go near it. It transpired that he did not know what grass was. Mrs Boden had brought him up indoors. It took us most of the summer to persuade that animal to walk on grass. I dug up turfs and put them in the mews; I put his food on them so that he had to walk across grass. It was fascinating to watch him trying to get that food without having to walk on it. He was very fond of his food, though, and he eventually gave in; but it was a long time before he would willingly go on grass and when he did finally move outside, he always preferred to take the long way round (via the path) rather than walk across the lawn. Having overcome his resistance, I gave him fresh turfs every day, scattering his food on them, and making sure that there were plenty of insects.

Mrs Boden had been giving him six ounces of food a day and he was rather fat and lethargic in comparison with our other wild animals. I gradually cut his food down, but I always made sure that he would never be short of natural food: while the birds were feeding on day-old chicks, he would never starve. We train kestrels which stay with us for any length of time like falcons, keeping them on blocks in the garden during the day and on perches at night.

The kestrels often discarded the stomachs (or yolks) of the day-old chicks which are their principal food; and it so happened that these yolks were the hedgehog's favourite food. He soon learned to associate their availability with my taking the birds in at night. When I took the first kestrel on to my fist, the hedgehog would amble out and follow me, walking to heel like an obedient gun dog, sniffing noisily at anything that seemed edible.

It was not in any way tame: that hedgehog was completely self-assured and self-opinionated. If a kestrel was still eating when he thought it should have dropped the food on the ground for him, he would sniff and chunter round the block until the bird gave up. He did not follow me round because he was tame: I was simply leading him to his favourite food. But if anyone came up with me, he would go back into his box and nothing would persuade him to come out.

We soon reached the stage where he was not ready to go back into the mews when I wanted to shut the door. I was a little concerned about this: we had three other hedgehogs which wandered round that part of the garden every night and I could not be sure that they would not pick a fight with this hand-reared one. It was about this time that it started to behave peculiarly, walking round and round in circles. I put it out in the garden but it still kept circling. Then it stopped and stayed absolutely motionless. Soon one of the wild hedgehogs appeared and started to walk in circles round him; then it stopped too. The two animals ambled off as if they had nothing whatsoever to do with each other. I could not understand the reason for this circling, nor for some of the other ways they behaved towards each other: moving backwards and forwards; remaining motionless face to face for minutes at a time. One day I sat down in the fields and made myself a hiding place in the hedge so that I could watch the wild hedgehogs without being seen. They do not come out until dusk and it was often difficult to distinguish them. When I first used to go nearer to get a better look they would curl up into a ball and stay like that so long that I gave up watching. The tractor driver used to come back down the lane as I got into position each evening. I do not think he ever did decide what I was doing. At first he used to say 'Goodnight,' when he saw me sitting in the hedge, but later he just drove past, glancing at me rather strangely out of the corner of his eye.

I discovered that when the hedgehogs in the garden behaved in an unusual way, the wild ones down the lane followed a very similar pattern. I decided that if the hand-reared hedgehog was behaving in exactly the same way as the wild ones, there was no need for me to protect it. John thought that I was being too slow with it: he fitted up a run outside for me. It was quite complicated, but it was fixed up so that the hedgehog could feed each evening, roam out into the garden and find its own way back without any of the stray cats getting into its box. I stayed up late for several nights to see that it was all right, and on those occasions I had the rare opportunity to see hedgehogs cover themselves with saliva. I thought they were ill at first: they would foam at the mouth, throw the saliva over their shoulders and spatter it down their spines. I had never seen this before although other people had told me about it. I could not think why a hedgehog should behave in this way – unless it is similar to a bird's habit of anting.

It seemed to be a real hedgehog year that year. The trouble is that when something happens that they do not like, they curl themselves up into a ball and lie still. In the countryside, when a stray dog or a farm tractor has menaced it there is little cause for concern; on the roads, it is a different matter altogether: the cars which have upset them carry on coming at the same speed and run them over. Hedgehogs, like any other animal, do have the capacity to learn: many of them will now run back to the grass when they see a car's lights approaching; but many hedgehogs are still killed on our roads each summer. The majority of the ones which are brought to us have been stunned; we try, wherever possible, to release them where they were picked up. Hedgehogs have their territories, too, and the males in particular can be very aggressive. One boar which I have watched seemed to spend half its life fighting other hedgehogs. What is not so widely known is that they are very loyal animals: when they pair they do so for life. This is another good reason for returning a hedgehog to its own territory.

All the other hedgehogs seemed to be pleased to return to the country; only the one which had been reared in captivity seemed contented with his lot. He would wander round the garden for half an hour, eat a couple of chicks and amble back through the small hole into his run, staying there until it was time for me to put his food in the next evening. He knew what he liked: cooked chicken, cheese and milk. If I did not put them out for him on time, he would chunter round the garden grumbling like an old man who has lost his tobacco pouch.

Then he decided that he liked apples. It had been a very windy day and they had been falling off the trees in the orchard. The hedgehog loved them, especially if they were bruised. One day he found a group of apples that were almost completely brown. He tucked into those as if he had not had a meal for days. He was so full up with apples that he could not walk properly. He staggered back to the run – but he could not get in. He made one or two attempts to squeeze through the hole, but he kept missing it and hitting his nose on the wire.

'He's drunk,' said John. 'Those rotten apples must be neat cider. He can't even stand.'

He did look a bit unsteady on his feet. I opened the lid and put him back in his box. The next night the same thing happened, so I put him to bed again. On the third night he followed me along the garden path and fell all the way down the steps, rolling himself into a ball as he felt himself falling so that he rolled a bit further still and finished up in the lavender bush. So I put him away again. This went on for a week. On the last two days, he found his way to the back door. When I went up to the top lawn on the eighth day, the hedgehog had pulled his nest to pieces. In the past he had been so careful with it; now there were bits of leaves and hay scattered all over the run.

'Are you sure it was your hedgehog you put in the run? He hasn't been fighting a stranger, has he?' John asked.

'I'm not sure.'

'We'd better look.'

We opened the box. I had put the hedgehog to bed on seven consecutive nights, or so I thought and, there, packed together like sardines, were seven hedgehogs.

'Now,' said John, 'which one's yours?'

I did not know.

They all looked exactly alike. They were all the same size and they all weighed between two and a half and two and three-quarter pounds.

'I know how I can tell,' I said confidently. 'Ours snores.'

They all seemed to be snoring. None of them were in any way disturbed by our looking at them. The only thing we could do was to remove the side of the run and let the hedgehogs decide which one lived with us. Four went straight away but three decided they were for the easy life. They all learned to chunter and grumble if their dish of food was not put out at the same time in the same spot every night.

Three days later, Mrs Bellamy came down and said, 'I've got your hedgehog in my garden. It won't let the cats have their milk so I have to put an extra dish out for it.'

Another lady in the village came and asked if I would take my hedgehog back because it had moved in with her. It was entering her house, sitting in the dog's dinner and not letting him get near it until it had eaten its fill. Two more people called to inform me that my hedgehog was in their garden and that they were having to feed it. Suddenly, the village seemed to be full of hedgehogs. The three that had taken over our garden had moved out of the run. I could not discover where they were sleeping but I knew that they had built other nests. I had seen them pulling hay together, and when I went out the next morning the hay had gone. Every evening they turned up for their meal at the same time and I knew when I had arrived late by the noise they were making.

Soon autumn was with us. One day, as the swallows were congregating ready to leave, the hedgehogs simply disappeared. They have appeared from time to time through the winter, all three of them, rooting out apples that have been buried under the falling leaves; but they have not come to me for food. They have completely ignored me when we have come across each other in the garden.

I wonder if they will turn up for their free meals again this year?

CHAPTER FIFTEEN: A Last Word

I wish I could say that every animal that comes to us returns to its own world without any trouble. Unfortunately, things are not as easy as that. Perhaps looking after sick wild animals and reintroducing them to their own environment sounds simple; but not every story is one of success.

About a third of those brought to us die; some of them as a result of their injuries, some because of the stress of being in captivity. Another third never reach the stage where we try to release them. This may be because they have not become fit enough; or it may be that they have been in captivity for so long that they have become used to the human situation, and would be unable to adapt to the wild one; or it may simply be that they have become too tame. In general, the last group either stays with us or goes to another centre which has better facilities for caring for them. Whenever possible, we try to breed from injured birds and release the young to the wild. We have had some success with this and know that some birds bred in our aviaries have themselves reared young in the wild.

Approximately one in every three animals that comes to the centre is reintroduced to the wild. It is difficult to say how many of them survive. When we first started and discovered all the difficulties and pitfalls of animal rehabilitation, we used to say that if we returned one creature successfully back to its natural life, all the effort and money we were spending would have been worth while. Now we are more ambitious: we like to think that the creature's return to the wild is complete; that it will look after itself in a natural environment; that it will be totally accepted by its own kind and that it will breed and rear its own young. Marking and ringing recoveries have shown that a number of our birds have achieved this aim and I doubt whether anyone can understand how John and I felt when we spent one evening watching a pair of barn owls feeding their young in the hollowed out ash tree in the full knowledge that they were both birds which we had released. They both had the mauve dye on their tails with which we had marked them.

It generally takes a long time for a creature which has been in captivity to become completely wild: between two months and two years for a tawny owl to go, between two weeks and nine months for a badger.

It is nearly a quarter of a century since we took in our first animal. In 1967, we released our thousandth bird and in 1968 our two hundredth animal. It has not all been easy but we have felt that it has been worth while. We have been disappointed when our commitment to the animals has obliged us to cancel a holiday or a trip; or when they have cost so much that we have run short of money. We have been upset when something has died that we thought should have been saved or when we have come across some example of unnecessary suffering: like the kingfisher's nest which a group of boys took home from a Derbyshire river without any understanding of how to look after them; or the buzzard which came to us in such a terrible state that we did not recognize it for what it was. Somebody had obviously kept it in captivity before they took it out into the countryside and had later discarded it. It did not have an entire feather on its body; its claws had been cut so far back that it was unable to perch.

Most of our callers are people like ourselves who find something in need and want to help it. Young John Wheeler is typical of many people we have met over the years. He was a little round-faced, twelve-year-old Yorkshire lad when he first came to see us. He phoned us up one day to say he had picked up a bird. Could we meet him at the station if he came down on the train? His Dad worked on the railway so he got cheap tickets.

When he got off the train there was not a sign of a bird – only a paper bag sticking out of his trouser pocket. He drew that out carefully and handed it over to John with the words, 'I bought it a ham sandwich on the station so it isn't hungry.'

When we opened the bag, a young blackbird cheeped out at us. It could not have been more than three weeks old and it was not a bit worried at having been confined in a paper bag.

Later that evening we went down to the station to see John off. As we stood waiting for the train, he turned to St John and said, 'I reckon you're the right luckiest kids alive. It's not that you live with animals, but you can help them. You can do something.'

When he had gone, St John said, 'He's right you know: we are lucky.'

We all are. I know that what we have done for animals which have come to us has been infinitesimally small in comparison with the numbers that are found in the wild. We have done what we have thought was right. I know that we have not always been successful in what we have set out to do and that, at times, the animals have caused a lot of pressure on the family but they, in their turn, have given us an immense amount of pleasure and a real sense of achievement. We have indeed been lucky.

CHILDREN'S BOOKS

0426 Target

Adventure

	Graeme Cook			
105087	COMMANDOS IN ACTION!	(illus)	(NF)	35p
	Terrance Dicks			
	THE MOUNTIES:			
110927	THE GREAT MARCH WEST			40p
	THE MOUNTIES:			
111052	MASSACRE IN THE HILLS			40p
	THE MOUNTIES:			
111133	WAR DRUMS OF THE BLACKFOOT			45p
	Rex Edwards			
105400	ARTHUR OF THE BRITONS			40p
	G. Krishnamurti			
103645	THE ADVENTURES OF RAMA			35p
	John Lucarotti			
11535X	OPERATION PATCH			45p

Animal Stories

	Judith M. Berrisford			
107004	SKIPPER AND SON		(illus)	35p
107195	SKIPPER AND THE RUNAWAY BOY		(illus)	35p
107276	SKIPPER'S EXCITING SUMMER			40p
	Molly Burkett			
111567	THAT MAD, BAD BADGER . . .		(NF)	35p
	Constance Taber Colby			
109899	A SKUNK IN THE FAMILY	(illus)	(NF)	45p
	G. D. Griffiths			
113675	ABANDONED!		(illus)	35p
	David Gross			
117549	THE BADGERS OF BADGER HILL			50p
	Sara Herbert			
109627	THE PONY PLOT			35p
109708	THE SECRET OF THE MISSING FOAL			35p
	Alex Lea			
107861	TEMBA DAWN, MY CALF			30p
	Joyce Stranger			
11017X	THE SECRET HERDS		(illus)	45p
	Alison Thomas			
115511	BENJI			40p

*Not for sale in Canada.

CHILDREN'S BOOKS

Fairy Fantasy

	Maria Gripe			
112288	**THE GLASSBLOWER'S CHILDREN**			45p

Girl's Romantic Fiction

	Ruth M. Arthur			
111648	**THE AUTUMN GHOSTS**			50p
111729	**THE CANDLEMAS MYSTERY**			45p*

Hobby Books (NF)

	Christopher Reynolds			
10823X	**CREATURES OF THE BAY**		(illus)	50p
100573	**THE POND ON MY WINDOW-SILL**		(illus)	30p
	David Shaw			
112369	**CRAFTS FOR GIRLS**			50p

0426 Life Stories

	John Rowland			
104013	**ROCKET TO FAME**	(NF)	(illus)	25p

Magic and Family Stories

	Nina Beachcroft			
103564	**WELL MET BY WITCHLIGHT**			30p
	Helen Cresswell			
	THE WHITE SEA HORSE			
108825	**and Other Sea Magic**		(illus)	35p
	Eleanor Estes			
107519	**THE WITCH FAMILY**		(illus)	50p
	Margaret Greaves			
10305X	**STONE OF TERROR**			30p
	Elizabeth Gundrey			
108906	**THE SUMMER BOOK**	(NF)	(illus)	45p
	Mollie Hunter			
113756	**THE WALKING STONES**			45p*
	Spike Milligan			
105672	**BADJELLY THE WITCH**		(illus)	60p
109546	**DIP THE PUPPY**		(illus)	60p
	Hilary Seton			
106989	**THE HUMBLES**		(illus)	50p
	THE NOEL STREATFIELD CHRISTMAS			
109112	**HOLIDAY BOOK**		(illus)	40p
	THE NOEL STREATFIELD EASTER			
109031	**HOLIDAY BOOK**		(illus)	45p
	THE NOEL STREATFIELD SUMMER			
105249	**HOLIDAY BOOK**		(illus)	50p

*Not for sale in Canada.

Wyndham Books are available from many booksellers and newsagents. If you have any difficulty please send purchase price plus postage on the scale below to:

Wyndham Cash Sales,
123 King Street,
London W6 9JG

While every effort is made to keep prices low, it is sometimes necessary to increase prices at short notice. Wyndham Books reserve the right to show new retail prices on covers which may differ from those advertised in the text or elsewhere.

Postage and Packing Rate

U.K. & Eire
One book 15p plus 7p per copy for each additional book ordered to a maximum charge of 57p.

These charges are subject to Post Office charge fluctuations.